AUTHOR'S BIOGRAPHY

David Wilson has a bachelor's degree in history from Miami University and a graduate degree in history from the University of Cincinnati. His writings have been published by educational institutes like Norwich University, Peregrine Academics, and Study.com. He lives in Denver.

CREDITS

COVER

(clockwise from top left) chris fennell/Shutterstock; kostasgr/Shutterstock; Quetzalcoatl1/Shutterstock; Lisa S./Shutterstock; Tupungato/Shutterstock; Tinnaporn Sathapornnanont/Shutterstock

INTERIOR

1, Carabiner/Dreamstime; 2-3, Kennyphotogallery/Dreamstime; 5, Dmitry Rukhlenko/Shutterstock; 9, Roomyana/Dreamstime; 10, Sohadiszno/Dreamstime; 11, Nick Fox/Shutterstock; 12, KaTeznik/Wikimedia Commons; 13, Africanway/iStock; 14, Demerzel21/Dreamstime; 15, DemarK/Shutterstock; 16, WitR/Shutterstock; 17, evenfh/Shutterstock; 18, trevor kittelty/Shutterstock; 19, Eddiemm/Wikimedia Commons; 20 (UP), Erik Kristensen/Wikimedia Commons; 20 (LO), Nick Hobgood/Wikimedia Commons; 21, Ylivdesign/Dreamstime; 22, Oleksandr Drozdov/Dreamstime; 23, Rui Serra Maia/Shutterstock; 24, Ttstudio/Shutterstock; 25, chomphunuts/Shutterstock; 26, Swedishnomad.com/Shutterstock; 27, Ahoerstemeier/Wikimedia Commons; 28, Elisa.rolle/Wikimedia Commons; 29, Pakin Songmor/Dreamstime; 30, Minyun Zhou/Dreamstime; 31 (UP), D Ramey Logan/Wikimedia Commons; 31 (LO), STARSsoft/Shutterstock; 32 (UP), artistVMG/Shutterstock; 32 (LO), Hecke01/Dreamstime; 33, Norbert Buchholz/Dreamstime; 34, saiko3p/Shutterstock; 35, Jennifer Barrow/Dreamstime; 36, Zharov Pavel/Shutterstock; 37, Minacarson/Dreamstime; 38, maziarz/Shutterstock; 39, Thegrimfandango/Dreamstime; 40, Hung Chung Chih/Shutterstock; 41, Alberto Molinero/Dreamstime; 42, RudyBalasko/iStock; 43, NeonJellyfish/iStock; 44, Carmenmurillo/Dreamstime; 45, Serkan OZBAY/Dreamstime; 46, DoraDalton/iStock; 47, SEYLUL06/iStock; 48, Iren Key/Shutterstock; 49, isitsharp/iStock; 50, Kamira/Shutterstock; 51, Tinamou/Dreamstime; 52, Tifonimages/Dreamstime; 53, Wikimedia Commons; 54, Sorin Colac/Dreamstime; 55 (UP), N1924/Shutterstock; 55 (LO), Mihai-bogdan Lazar/Dreamstime; 56 (UP), xeni4ka/iStock; 56 (LO), Janko Bartolec/Dreamstime; 57, Yana Kravchenko/Dreamstime; 58, Junior Braz/Shutterstock; 59, Robert Hoetink/Shutterstock; 60, ESB Professional/Shutterstock; 61, Zurijeta/Shutterstock; 62, Ignatius Tan/Shutterstock; 63, Per-Olow Anderson/Wikimedia Commons; 64, Fdebbi/Wikimedia Commons; 65, Wiktor Wojtas/Dreamstime; 66, MrPhotoMania/Shutterstock; 67 (UP), nmessana/iStock; 67 (LO), VanderWolf Images/Shutterstock; 68 (UP), Vivienne Sharp Heritage Images/Newscom; 68 (LO), Phooey/iStock; 69, Godruma/Dreamstime; 70, Vadim Petrakov/Shutterstock; 71, Cezary Wojtkowski/iStock; 72, Songquan Deng/Shutterstock; 73, Roman Tiraspolsky/Shutterstock; 74, Sopotnicki/Shutterstock; 75, aaron rhodes/Shutterstock; 76, Mike Clegg/Dreamstime; 77, Maxcrepory/Dreamstime; 78, Viniko2010/Dreamstime; 79 (UP), Diego Cervo/Shutterstock; 79 (LO), Edinaldo Maciel/Shutterstock; 80 (UP), Rafael Ben Ari/Dreamstime; 80 (LO), Ton Koene / VWPics/Newscom; 81, Yehor Vlasenko/Dreamstime; 82, Max421/Dreamstime; 83, Mishkacz/Dreamstime; 84, Rafael Ben Ari/Dreamstime; 85, matiascausa/Shutterstock; 86, maloff/Shutterstock; 87, maloff/Shutterstock; 88, Stbernardstudio/Dreamstime; 89, Vichean Jintakaweekul/Shutterstock; 90, saiko3p/Shutterstock; 91 (UP), Sbostock/Dreamstime; 91 (LO), Ralf Broskvar/Shutterstock; 92 (UP), Steve Shattuck/Wikimedia Commons; 92 (LO), RYOSUE/Shutterstock

INDEX

Abu Simbel temples (Egypt), 62–63
Agadez, Niger, 18
Al-Haram Mosque (Mecca), 60–61
ancient structures, 22–23, 36–37, 41, 46–47, 62–63, 68, 70–71, 74–75, 78
Angkor Wat (Cambodia), 26–27
architects, 24, 34–35, 38–39, 40, 43, 44, 53, 56, 59, 77, 79, 82–83

Bab al-Wastani (Baghdad gate), 68
Bandiagara Escarpment (Mali), 15
Barcelona Modernism (Spain), 34–35
Beni Hammad Fort (Algeria), 64
Boudhanath Stupa (Nepal), 29
Britam Tower (Kenya), 19
Buddhist wats and stupas, 26–27, 29
burial and afterlife, buildings for, 15, 30, 91, 92
Burj Khalifa (Dubai, UAE), 58–59

Carlton Centre (South Africa), 14
Casco Viejo (Panama), 79
Castillo San Filipe del Morro (Puerto Rico), 54
castles and palaces, 16, 31, 42, 43, 56, 67
cathedrals and churches, 11, 34–35, 48–49, 51, 53, 79, 88, 90
Chichén Itzá pyramids (Mexico), 78
Christ the Redeemer (Brazil), 48–49
cities, ruins of, 17, 46–47, 64, 70–71, 74–75, 78, 86–87
cliff dwellings, 15, 74–75
CN (Canadian National) Tower (Toronto), 76
Coliseum (Rome, Italy), 41
colonialism, influences of, 10–11, 50–51, 53, 54, 79, 90
Concha Acústica (Nicaragua), 79
Corinthia Hotel (Libya), 20

Devon House (Jamaica), 55
Dome of the Rock (Israel), 67
domes, 29, 30, 66–67, 77, 80, 91, 92

Edo Castle (Japan), 31
Eiffel Tower (Paris, France), 40
El Jem Amphitheater (Tunisia), 68
Emerald Towers (Kazakhstan), 31
Empire State Building (New York City), 72–73
estancias (for cowboys of Argentina), 56
European influences, 11, 16, 33, 88

Fasil Ghebbi (Ethiopia), 16
forts and fortresses, 10–11, 22–23, 54, 64

"Gaddafi's Egg" (Libya), 20
Gaudí, Antoni (Barcelona), 34–35
Gherkin building (London), 38–39
Golden Gate Bridge (San Francisco), 80
Gran Torre (Chile), 52
Great Wall of China, 22–23
Great Zimbabwe National Monument, 17
Guggenheim Museum (New York City), 77
Guggenheim Museum Bilbao (Spain), 44

Hagia Sophia (Turkey), 66
haus tambaran (Papua New Guinea), 92
historic districts, 28, 50–51, 79, 90
House of Wonders (Zanzibar), 11

igloos (Inuit peoples), 80
Inca Empire (Peru), 46–47
Intramuros (Philippines), 90

Jabreen Castle (Oman), 67

Louvre and Pyramid (Paris, France), 43

Machu Picchu (Peru), 46–47
medieval buildings, 12–13, 17, 42, 61, 68, 90
Mesa Verde (Colorado), 74–75
Mesoamerica, 70–71, 78
modern design, 19, 34–35, 38–39, 43, 44, 65
mosques and shrines, 11, 12–13, 18, 60–61, 66, 67
mud bricks and towers, 12–13, 18, 20

Nan Madol (Micronesia), 86–87
Neuschwanstein Castle (Germany), 42
Notre Dame Cathedral (Haiti), 53

Old Havanna (Cuba), 50–51

Palacio Salvo (Uruguay), 56
Parthenon (Athens, Greece), 36–37
Pei, I. M., 43
Petronas Towers (Malaysia), 24–25
Polynesian ingenuity, 87
Port Town (Fiji), 88
postmodern design, 24, 59, 77
pyramids, 43, 62, 70–71, 78

Q1 Tower (Australia), 91

Royal Exhibition Building (Australia), 92
Ryugyong Hotel (North Korea), 32

Shard building (London), 38–39
skyscrapers, 14, 19, 24–25, 31, 32, 38–39, 52, 58–59, 65, 72–73, 91
Sky Tower (New Zealand), 84–85
St. Mary's Basilica (New Zealand), 91
Stone Town (Zanzibar), 10–11
Sydney Opera House (Australia), 82–83

Taj Mahal (India), 30
takienta (Koutammakou, Togo), 20
Tanah Lot (Indonesia), 89
Tanjong Pagar (Singapore), 28
temples, 26–27, 36–37, 62–63, 89
Teotihuacan (Mexico), 70–71
Timbuktu (Africa), 12–13
Tornado Tower (Qatar), 65
towers, 18–19, 20, 24–25, 31, 40, 52, 58–59, 65, 76, 84–85, 91
treehouses (Amazon rain forest), 55

Utzon, Jørn, 82–83

World Heritage Sites, 12, 23, 29, 34, 92

yurts (Mongolia), 32

https://www.metropolismag.com/. Famous for identifying young, up-and-coming architects, *Metropolis* magazine and its digital platform comment on many aspects of the profession, including education and sustainability.

https://www.studyarchitecture.com/. For students interested in a career as an architect, Study Architecture provides valuable advice, job placement opportunities, and rankings of schools to help launch a professional career.

FURTHER READING & INTERNET RESOURCES

BOOKS

Borden, Daniel, Jerzy Elzanowski, Joni Taylor, and Stephanie Tuerk. *Architecture: A World History*. New York: Harry N. Abrams, 2008. This illustrated work features some 600 different buildings across space and time, from the ancient to the modern.

Ching, Francis D.K. *Architecture: Form, Space, and Order*. Hoboken, NJ: John Wiley & Sons, 2014. One of the most practical and often used books about architecture, this text introduces students to the basic and important concepts.

Kushner, Marc. *The Future of Architecture in 100 Buildings*. New York: Simon & Schuster, 2015. Inspired by a TED Talk, this book looks at the future of construction and design by identifying next-generation buildings.

McAlester, Virginia Savage. *A Field Guide to American Houses: The Definitive Guide to Identifying and Understanding America's Domestic Architecture*. New York: Knopf, 2015. With a wide array of historical trends and styles, this guide to American architecture provides insight on structures from coast to coast.

Roth, Leland, and Amanda C. Roth Clark. *Understanding Architecture: Its Elements, History, and Meaning*. 3rd ed. Boulder, CO: Westview Press, 2014. This survey of Western architecture is useful for students interested in learning more about the foundations of architecture.

WEB SITES

https://www.architecturaldigest.com/. Arguably the most famous architecture magazine in the United States, *Architectural Digest* covers topics from buildings to interior design to real estate itself, offering students and professionals alike an excellent source for news.

https://www.architecturalrecord.com/. With a 125-year history of news and opinion on global architecture, *Architectural Record* provides updates on projects, competitions, new designs, and other trends throughout the world.

https://www.curbed.com/. Unlike global-facing architecture news sites, Curbed offers a far more local take on buildings. Readers can find projects going up in their neighborhood and insights into their own homes.

https://www.dezeen.com/. The UK-based architecture magazine *Dezeen* not only publishes articles about buildings and renovations but also created its own Dezeen Awards to highlight successes throughout the architecture world.

THE SPIRITS OF NEW GUINEA'S HAUS TAMBARAN

The Sepik peoples of Papua New Guinea build a structure called a *haus tambaran* in the center of their villages. These spirit houses, made of wood and thatch, can rise as high as 75 feet (22.8 m), typically using an A-frame design to carry the weight and provide cover for several dozen people. A spirit house will feature the totems of each clan of the Sepik, with ornate decorations of ancestors' faces around the walls. The Sepik believe they can commune with the spirits of ancestors in a *haus tambaran*, gaining insight from long-deceased relatives. When they must reach a political decision, members gather in the spirit house and sit around a debating stool, hitting it with large leaf clusters to emphasize a point.

The haus tambaran *is typically an A-frame design with ornate decorations of ancestors' faces around the walls.*

THE SIGHTS OF THE ROYAL EXHIBITION BUILDING, MELBOURNE

The Royal Exhibition Building is surrounded by the Carlton Gardens, which are just as beautiful as the building's architecture.

In 1880, Australia hosted an international exhibition to demonstrate its progress to the world. The Royal Exhibition Building, constructed to serve as a home for the show, remains standing today. It is a beautiful work of Victorian Italian Renaissance architecture, featuring an elaborate dome rising 200 feet (61 m) into the air. The surrounding Carlton Gardens are just as striking, with 64 acres devoted to Australian flora. Although the building was constructed for the 1880 exhibition, it has played host to some 50 other exhibitions throughout its lifetime, and today is a World Heritage Site.

LIVING THE Q1 LIFE

Australia's Q1 Tower is the largest residential building in the country, as well as the Southern Hemisphere, standing over 1,100 feet (335 m) tall. Located in the city of Gold Coast, it soars above the beautiful eastern coastline near Australia's Great Barrier Reef. Construction on the skyscraper began in 2002 and concluded in 2005 under the leadership of the Australian architectural firm Sunland Group, requiring 2.5 million man-hours to complete. The upsweeping curves of the tower's top are a stylistic nod to the Sydney Opera House, whereas ribbons of aluminum curve around the superstructure to create a pleasant-looking motif.

The Q1 Tower required 2.5 million man-hours to complete. It is the largest residential building in both Australia and the Southern Hemisphere.

ST. MARY'S BASILICA, NEW ZEALAND

St. Mary's Basilica features a Baroque design and a magnificent copper dome.

The southernmost Catholic basilica in the world can be found in Invercargill, New Zealand (itself one of the southernmost cities in the world). St. Mary's Basilica, completed in 1904, tends to the Catholic faithful of the city and earned a spot on the New Zealand National Register of Historic Places in 1980. It features a Baroque design with a magnificent copper dome, built by the architect Francis Petre. Despite its relatively small size, rising just 100 feet into the air, the bright red and cream coloration, as well as the stained-glass windows (some of the only stained glass in southern New Zealand) makes it visually striking. It is part of the larger Catholic diocese of Dunedin in New Zealand.

OCEANIA

ENTER INTRAMUROS, PHILIPPINES

We think of Spanish colonization as having taken place in the Americas, yet one of the most lucrative Spanish overseas colonies were the islands of the Philippines, named after Philip II of Spain. For centuries, the Spanish managed a spice and silk trade from the city of Manila. Their legacy is reflected in Intramuros, a walled area (*intramuros* means "within the walls") containing the historic district of Manila, with buildings that date back some 500 years to the first colonization.

The Spanish designed Intramuros in 1521 as a small city on a simple grid near Manila Bay. From here, their administration set up trade and spread Christianity. The wealth of historical buildings reflect this process: the Plaza Mayor (main square), Ayuntamiento (city hall), Plazo Santo Tomas (home to the first university in the Philippines), and the fantastic Manila Cathedral. The threat of attack from outsiders meant that Intramuros was also well protected with cannon and moats.

Intramuros's fantastic Cathedral.

The shrine of Tanah Lot, built out of rock escarpments, has been thrust into the Pacific Ocean. During low tide, the shrine is accessible by a narrow land bridge.

LOTS TO SEE AT TANAH LOT, INDONESIA

Indonesia today is a Muslim-majority nation, boasting a larger population of Muslims than any other nation in the world. However, the shrine of Tanah Lot reflects the history and importance of Hindu communities that came to the island of Bali for pilgrimage and prayer. The Tanah Lot shrine sits on the southern tip of Bali, built out of the rock escarpments that thrust into the Pacific Ocean.

Tanah Lot means "land in the sea," and the temple is indeed a slice of land in the sea, sitting atop a rock formation whose edges have been eroded over thousands of years. Today it remains standing, only connected by a narrow land bridge at low tide. Legend holds that a Hindu priest traveled to Bali in 1489 to spread his religion. He arrived at Tanah Lot and established the shrine to honor the sea god Baruna. A local village chief became angered at the priest and tried to attack him; the priest merely meditated on a large rock, shifting it out to sea, while his garments turned into sea snakes that attacked anyone who dared come near. The chief pledged his allegiance and was awarded a ceremonial dagger, which remains in the shrine to this day.

A PORT OF CALL IN PORT TOWN, FIJI

Most visitors who come to Fiji do so for the gorgeous tropical reefs and sandy beaches. Many may be surprised to find that this island nation has much more history on hand, however. Levuka Port Town is the historical district of Fiji on the eastern side of the main island, built in the early 1800s as a variety of outsiders—Americans, British, Dutch, and Japanese—all came to Fiji and started a new life.

Port Town features many important nineteenth-century buildings, like the former Parliament house, the Morris Hedstrom bond store, Sacred Heart Cathedral, Royal Hotel, and Captain Robbie's Bungalow. Nearby are two preserved villages that predate colonization, Totoga and Nasau. Port Town is unique in that the indigenous peoples outnumbered the foreign colonists, meaning that the architecture blends both European and native elements.

The Sacred Heart Cathedral in Levuka Port Town, Fiji.

Inside the ruins of Nan Madol.

their underlings and, at times, even practicing cannibalism. Nan Madol was their capital city, though the Saudeleur society collapsed about 400 years ago.

Nan Madol today is a subject of fascination for architects and historians alike. It's been called the Venice of the Pacific, based on its incredible construction on a reef rather than on land. The Saudeleur built walls of giant black basalt stones, stacking rocks of different diameters. Legend holds that two sorcerers built the structures with the help of a massive dragon, although radiocarbon dating suggests that the stonework was part of a larger Polynesian pattern of building, similar to another archaeological site on Lelu Island (built on land, rather than a coral reef).

Polynesian Transportation

How did people get from mainland Asia and Australia to the faraway islands of the South Pacific? Polynesian seafaring remains one of the great achievements of humanity, especially given the relative lack of technology in many Polynesian societies. Rafts, canoes, catamarans, and other boats could make it across thousands of miles of the Pacific, using nothing but wind power and navigating with nothing but the stars to guide them. Some anthropologists hypothesize that Polynesian peoples made it as far as South America in boats made of simple wood and thatch.

NAN MADOL: THE CITY BUILT ON CORAL REEFS

Micronesia, as you may suspect from the name, is one of the smallest countries in the world, spread across some 600 islands in the South Pacific. With so little space, building materials can be in short supply. The people of Pohnpei Island, located about 2,000 miles (3,218 km) northeast of Australia, decided to overcome this obstacle by building on a coral reef instead of on dry land. About 1,000 years ago they constructed the city of Nan Madol atop a coral reef. It's still the only civilization in history to do so. Although the city has since fallen into ruins, its structures remain standing, a testament to the architectural genius of the Saudeleur civilization in its heyday. The name Nan Madol itself means "the space between," referring to the seawater canals that divided each structure.

The ruins of Nan Madol feature a number of mysteries. Its stone structures and columns appear far too heavy for the Saudeleur inhabitants of the island, who lacked work animals like horses, to be able to move them. What's more, unlike other ruins from Egypt to Mexico, Nan Madol has no carvings, artworks, inscriptions, hieroglyphs, or other bits of communication that could help archaeologists better understand their daily lives. What little we do know about the Saudeleur is that they were master builders and could be particularly cruel, demanding harsh tribute from

Seawater canals divide each structure in Nan Madol.

The Sky Tower is not only the tallest structure in New Zealand but also the tallest BASE jump in the country. People often partake in thrilling tasks like free falls and bungee jumping.

up to 125 miles per hour (201 km/h), expected to hit New Zealand once every 1,000 years, which would sway the tower by only about a single yard (1 m). Eight separate concrete "legs" provide the stability needed for the tower to remain standing in the face of these natural disasters.

The Sky Tower holds many New Zealand records, including being the tallest building in the country, having the tallest observation deck in the country, and having the tallest BASE jump opportunity in the country, with a 600-foot (182 m) free fall. The tower makes up the keystone of the Auckland entertainment complex, featuring two hotels, two dozen bars and restaurants, a movie theater, and a casino. About half a million visitors per year take the elevator to one of the two observation decks, where they can see as far as 50 miles on a clear day, allowing them to spot Auckland's nearest volcano, Mt. Eden.

TOUCHING THE SKY IN THE SKY TOWER

The Sky Tower is the tallest structure in New Zealand.

The Sky Tower is New Zealand's tallest structure, coming in at over 1,000 feet (305 m), which also makes it the tallest freestanding (not requiring a foundation) structure in the Southern Hemisphere. Construction began on this communications tower, located in Auckland on the northern island, in 1994 and was completed in 1997 under the leadership of architects at Craig Craig Moller. It is the host of the largest FM radio transmitter in the world and also houses weather instruments used by the National Weather Service.

Construction of the Sky Tower required many safeguards against earthquakes, a persistent threat in New Zealand due to the island nation's location against the Pacific continental plate. An earthquake measuring 7.0 on the Richter scale would not affect the tower, and even an 8.0 earthquake (equivalent to some of the most devastating earthquakes in history) would not be able to topple it. What's more, the Sky Tower can resist hurricane-strength winds of

The concrete shells were the biggest challenge in the construction of the Opera House.

One of the biggest challenges in the construction of the Sydney Opera House was the concrete shells themselves. The design and mathematics of building them from scratch proved to be too much. Engineers had to construct large spheres from concrete and then cut out the wings individually to make certain they had proper structural integrity. Construction began in 1959, but a major controversy erupted in 1966 when the Australian government believed the project was taking too much time and money. They sacked Utzon, and despite public marches to reinstate the Danish architect, Utzon left Australia and never saw the completed structure.

Peter Hall took over the design of the building, and construction ended in 1973. Today, the Sydney Opera House receives 8 million visitors per year, and many performing arts groups consider it a great honor to be invited to sing, dance, or act on its stages, which host 1,500 events per year.

SYDNEY OPERA HOUSE: ART INSIDE AND OUT

Without a doubt, the most famous building in all of Australia is the opera house that sits near the harbor mouth of the nation's largest city. The Sydney Opera House, as the name suggests, is one of the world's best known performing arts centers, with a beautiful fan-shell roof design that is instantly recognizable.

The Sydney Opera House reflects the creative genius of Danish architect Jørn Utzon, who won a competition in 1957 to design the new building. At the time, Utzon had no major credits to his name, but his bold vision for the opera house won over the judges of the international competition and instantly made him one of the world's most famous architects. At a time when architectural orthodoxy preached rectangular cube buildings, Utzon's unique concept of a structure that had waving, nonparallel curves allowed him to stand out from the crowd.

The Sydney Opera House is one of the world's best known performing arts centers.

CHAPTER 7 OCEANIA

The warm, tropical islands that dot the Pacific may afford their inhabitants such lovely surroundings that they require little more than a small house of wood, grass, and stone. By contrast, the tropical storms and earthquakes that occur around the Rim of Fire may necessitate much stronger, sturdier places to live and work.

A RED BRIDGE OF GOLD

Perhaps the most famous bridge in the world, San Francisco's Golden Gate Bridge joins the San Francisco promontory with Marin County across the bay. At the time of its opening in 1937, it was both the tallest and the longest suspension bridge in the world, at just over a mile (1.6 km) in length and 750 feet (22.8 m) in height. It carries the famous Route 1 from south to north across its red-steel Art Deco design. The bridge features its own walking path for those who wish to go across it on foot, rather than by car, and is one of the most famous symbols of San Francisco and California today.

The Golden Gate Bridge was made with a red-steel Art Deco design. It connects Route 1 from south the north.

KEEP COOL IN AN IGLOO

The Inuit people do not build with traditional materials. Instead, they build with snow and ice, constructing igloos from big bricks of snow.

The Inuit peoples of the far north reside in Alaska, Canada, and Greenland, where there's little building material to be had. Without timber, stones, steel, concrete, or glass, their traditional structure makes use of what the Inuit do have in abundance: snow and ice. They construct igloos from big bricks of snow, carefully layering them in a dome that has a hole in the center for smoke to escape. The entrance to an igloo can be below the snow itself, forcing visitors to crawl through. Once they stand up, however, they notice that the interior temperature is far warmer than the Arctic outside, especially because the Inuit line igloos with animal furs for sitting and sleeping.

VIEJO, THE OLD

One of the oldest city centers in Central America is appropriately named Casco Viejo, or "Old Helmet," found in modern Panama. Although Spanish colonization reached Central America, the thick forests and hordes of mosquitoes meant that they didn't spend much time putting down roots. One exception was in Panama, where it's easiest to cross from the Atlantic to the

The Metropolitan Cathedral in Casco Viejo stands out with two stone towers and huge wooden doors.

Pacific. The Spanish began to build the fantastic Metropolitan Cathedral in 1668 CE but did not complete it for another 130 years. Two stone towers, which feature mother-of-pearl finish from Pearl Island, flank its huge wooden doors, whereas the spacious interior of the cathedral has a solid marble altar.

LISTEN TO THE CONCHA ACÚSTICA

The Concha Acústica is a popular, and unique, space in Nicaragua for symphonies.

In the plaza near the historic district of Managua, Nicaragua, you'll see a structure that quite clearly is not historic. Named for the giant shell that it resembles, the white Concha Acústica rises from the concrete in a waving, semispiral pattern meant to accentuate the music that is played on the nearby orchestra stage. Standing 75 feet (23 m) tall and designed by architect Glen Small, the Concha seems to wave to visitors. Though parts of it have been dismantled from the original design, it remains a striking contrast to the rest of the plaza and is a popular place for an evening symphony.

NORTH AMERICA

THE PYRAMIDS OF CHICHÉN ITZÁ, MEXICO

The Mayan peoples of Central America left a number of legacies of their civilization behind after its collapse about 1,000 years ago. None are more impressive than the standing city of Chichén Itzá, one of the most well-preserved archaeological sites in the world. Built about 1,500 years ago next to a pair of *cenote* well springs (the name of the city means "at the edge of the well"), Chichén Itzá grew to be a major center of religious and political power. The Mayan city is dominated by El Castillo, the great pyramid, built in perfect symmetry of 91 steps on each of its four sides. Add up all these steps, plus the one on top for the temple, and you get 365, the number of days in the year.

Chichén Itzá features many fascinating structures. An ancient arena was the home of a Mesoamerican ball game in which participants bounced a rubber ball through a hoop; losers may have been sacrificed. An observation tower provided readings for astronomers, who built a calendar that still remains practical and accurate. Finally, a series of hieroglyphic carvings throughout the city tell stories of history and religion, helping to understand the city's rise to power, although not the mystery behind its abandonment about 600 years ago.

The Chichén Itzá houses El Castillo, the great pyramid.

Inside New York's Guggenheim Museum, a spiral ramp rises to meet the building's domed ceiling.

GUGGENHEIM'S GREAT MUSEUM

The wealthy Guggenheim family endowed a series of art museums around the world, hoping to build structures that would be as famous on the outside as their art would be on the inside. The most well known, and well studied, of these museums is the modern art museum located in Manhattan, New York City. Designed by Frank Lloyd Wright, by far the most famous architect in American history, the Solomon R. Guggenheim Museum's post-Modern style may resemble a stack of dishes, but it also features many impressive design choices.

    A spiral ramp within the Guggenheim rises to meet the building's domed ceiling. The museum has an open design, hoping to meld together art and architecture for visitors to appreciate both simultaneously. Although there are some rooms for collections, the majority of works hang on the walls as the ramp winds upward, creating a sense of constant movement. The art museum offers tours of its collections, of course, but it also offers architectural tours for those interested in the design of the building itself.

THE CN TOWER: CANADA'S ROOF

No trip to Toronto can be complete with a visit to the CN (Canadian National) Tower, the massive structure that soars 1,800 feet (548 m) above the Toronto skyline on the shores of Lake Ontario. Famous for its central bulge that allows visitors to see for miles in every direction on clear days, the CN Tower was the tallest tower in the world up until 2009, when the Burj Khalifa overtook its prowess. It remains the tallest structure in the Western Hemisphere, however, and about 2 million visitors per year come to see the view from the top.

This communications tower provides radio and television signals to the 6 million inhabitants of Toronto, by far Canada's largest city, which became necessary as Toronto built more skyscrapers that interfered with those signals. John Andrews Architects began planning for construction to begin in 1973, finishing three years later.

The CN Tower is a communications tower that provides radio and television signals to the 6 million people of Toronto.

To navigate through the varying levels of the cliff dwellings, the Pueblo people used ladders.

Constructed from simple mud, straw, and ash, the Mesa Verde buildings represent the pinnacle of Pueblo civilization—a people who lived in the area starting about 1,500 years ago and moved below the clifftops about 800 years ago. In fact, archaeologists suggest that more people lived in Mesa Verde in its heyday than live in the Four Corners area today. Corn crops provided the main staple, and irrigation came from rain running off the tops of cliffs. Other foods, including beans, squash, turkey, and peppers, complemented the Pueblo diet.

The story of Mesa Verde, however, finishes on a tragic note. For some reason, the Pueblo people abandoned these great structures. Drought remains the most common blame for the decline of their civilization—climate scientists estimate that by about 1300 CE the area was too dry for farming, forcing the Pueblo to move farther to the south in search of new opportunities. Today, Mesa Verde is a national park that showcases not only the fantastic cliff dwellings but also the progression of Pueblo civilization from aboveground dwellings to underground kivas to the final cities built below the cliff overhangs.

GREEN TABLE: THE STORY OF MESA VERDE

The first Spanish explorers to visit the southwestern United States came in search of the fabled Seven Cities of Gold. They didn't find gold, but they surveyed many areas around the northwestern United States and discovered inhabitants who had built fantastic cities from overhanging cliffs. The Spanish named this region Mesa Verde, which simply means "green table," because the clifftop vegetation reminded them of colored furniture. The more they explored, the more mysteries they found.

The abandoned cities of Mesa Verde in southwestern Colorado have been a source of intrigue for centuries. Home to the ancestral Pueblo people, these were some of the largest human settlements west of the Mississippi, with each cliff-dwelling community capable of housing dozens or even hundreds of people.

Although abandoned, the cliff-dwelling communities of the Pueblo people are still intact.

Visitors to the Empire State Building can make their way to the top of the building and view the city from its observation decks.

ever climbed. While most people assume the building takes its name from New York (called the Empire State), it in fact derives from the fact that Empire State Inc., a business in the early 1900s, purchased the property rights to develop the skyscraper. Americans followed the progress of the construction as the building competed with the Chrysler Building for the title of the world's tallest building, constructing up an average of four floors per week.

    Two observation towers make the Empire State Building a very popular attraction for New York tourists, and 4 million people per year ride the elevators up to the high floors to look over the famous Manhattan skyline. To the north lies Central Park and to the south lies the Financial District. It's not just appreciated by visitors, either. The American Institute of Architects named it their favorite piece of architecture in 2007, beating out other famous skyscrapers like Chicago's Sears Tower. The Empire State Building became a national landmark in 1986, and in 2019 it ranked as the fifth tallest building in the United States.

STAND ATOP THE EMPIRE STATE BUILDING

The United States has more skyscrapers than any other nation in the Western Hemisphere, and the Empire State Building is certainly the most famous of them all. Built in the iconic Art Deco style of the Roaring Twenties (although it was finished in 1931), the Empire State Building stood as the tallest building in the world for 40 years and became an iconic symbol of New York City and the United States itself. Its silhouette alone is easily recognizable by many Americans, while many of the black-and-white photographs taken during its construction have also become famous.

Everything about the Empire State Building is big. It stands nearly 1,500 feet (457 m) tall, boasts 86 stories, and is the only building that King Kong

The Empire State Building is one of the most recognizable buildings in the New York City skyline.

A Moon Pyramid in Teotihuacan.

because the massive mounds on the sides of the avenue looked like tombs to the first European colonists who discovered the city.

During the seventh century, an intense fire destroyed much or all of the city, and its inhabitants abandoned it. Nevertheless, Teotihuacan's fantastic architecture continued to inspire for many years after its end. The Aztec claimed common ancestry with the people who lived in Teotihuacan (although they migrated to central Mexico from the northeastern coast) and used their example to build their own massive pyramid structures in the capital city of Tenochtitlan, though none of them survive in the same condition as the Teotihuacan pyramids do.

Mesoamerican Engineering

One stereotypical view of Native American civilizations is that they never built anything more complex than a tepee. This, however, totally ignores the major achievements of civilizations like the Aztec, Maya, and inhabitants of Teotihuacan. The Aztec in particular proved to be master builders. They constructed aqueducts from mountain streams to flood the Mexico City valley, forming a man-made lake that they then built a city on top of. In 1500 CE their capital, Tenochtitlan, was likely the largest city in the world.

TAKE A TRIP TO THE AVENUE OF THE DEAD IN TEOTIHUACAN

When we think of Mesoamerica, we typically think of the Aztec, who famously sacrificed people to the gods and built massive pyramids. Yet both of these cultural legacies predate the Aztec by centuries. The ancient city of Teotihuacan pays homage to the prowess of Mesoamerican civilization. It was constructed anywhere from 1300 to 1900 years ago, with an entire city structure that remains standing long after its abandonment.

Located about 25 miles (40 km) to the north of Mexico City, Teotihuacan is not Aztec, nor is it Mayan. Indeed, we're not entirely sure exactly who built it, although at its height between 100 BCE and 650 CE some evidence suggests that multiple ethnic groups inhabited the area, with a population between 25,000 and 125,000, which would have made it one of the largest cities in the world during its prime. Teotihuacan features many elements of Mesoamerican culture, such as massive pyramids built for gods of the sun and moon, constructed in a style called *talud-tablero* that incorporates a foundation and a large overhang to build separate layers. In the center of the city is the Avenue of the Dead, a huge plaza that was doubtless used for commerce, religious ceremonies, and political announcements. It earned its name

The ancient city of Teotihuacan, which was at its height between 100 BCE and 650 CE, is one of the architectural marvels of the world.

CHAPTER 6 NORTH AMERICA

Some of the most well-known buildings in the world can be found in North American cities like New York and Chicago. The overall architecture of the continent, however, is far more nuanced than the skyscrapers that line the biggest cities of the United States and includes adaptions to survive in places from the High Arctic to the Sonoran Desert.

THE GATES OF BAGHDAD

The Bab al-Wastani is the last standing gate built by the Abbasid caliph in the eighth century.

Humans have inhabited the area that today is central Iraq for thousands, and perhaps tens of thousands, of years. Yet the city itself dates back to the eighth century when the Abbasid caliph constructed a wall with four gates. Of these four gates, just one remains, the Bab al-Wastani (which simply means "Western Gate"), and the city has long since expanded past it. Nevertheless, the Bab al-Wastani and surrounding medieval structures like the mausoleum of Sheikh Umar provide crucial insight into the architecture of the era. Restoration efforts have faltered due to ongoing conflict in Iraq, even though the gate, bridges, and fortifications have not been affected by the wars.

TAKE IN A SHOW AT EL JEM, TUNISIA

The El Jem Amphitheater of Tunisia may not be as famous as the Coliseum of Rome; however, it also was built by the Romans. The amphitheater stands on African sands rather than a foundation, yet the majority of the structure is still intact in several sections.

While the El Jem Amphitheater of Tunisia is nowhere near as well known as the Coliseum of Rome, it's nearly as large and much better preserved. Built by the ancient Romans in 238, the amphitheater is famous for several reasons, including the fact that it has no foundations and thus stands freely on the shifting African sands. Capable of fitting 35,000 spectators, El Jem is almost perfectly intact in several sections, including the outer wall and the arena itself. The Romans put on the same shows, from plays to gladiator contests to wild beast fights, in El Jem that they would have done in Rome itself.

JABREEN CASTLE, OMAN

Many castles built throughout the world functioned for defense, keeping enemies out and friends in. The Jabreen Castle of Oman was different: Constructed in the late 1600s, it reflects Imam Bil'arab bin Sultan's wish to create a legacy of peace and art

The Jabreen Castle stands three stories tall and features calligraphy worked into the stone.

in a time without strife. The castle stands three stories tall and features a variety of different rooms: a library, courtroom, dining hall, meeting rooms, reception halls, and classrooms. Like many other famous Islamic buildings, it too displays calligraphy worked into the stone. Its most famous room, the Sun and Moon Hall, has intricately decorated walls and windows that catch the eye.

A ROCKY PLACE IN ISRAEL: THE DOME OF THE ROCK

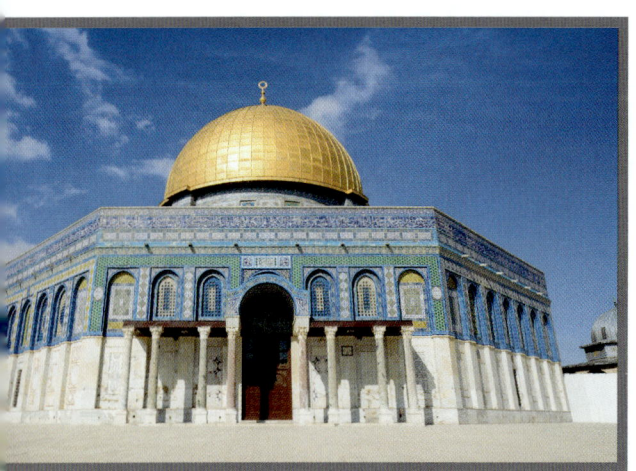

The Dome of the Rock stands out in Jerusalem's skyline with its golden roof. The building is one of the oldest works of Islamic architecture in the world.

Jerusalem represents one of the holiest sites in each of the three Abrahamic religions—Judaism, Christianity, and Islam. One of the most famous buildings in Jerusalem is the Dome of the Rock, an Islamic shrine built in 691 by Caliph Abd al-Malik, named because it stands atop the Foundation Stone believed to be the place where God created Adam and Eve. It's one of the oldest works of Islamic architecture in the world, an octagonal structure with perhaps the first dome known to the Muslim world—a design that would come to dominate Islamic mosques and palaces for centuries.

THE ENDURING HAGIA SOPHIA, TURKEY

Istanbul, Turkey, is a city that has changed names and ownership several times in its history. One thing that has remained over the centuries, however, is the beautiful Hagia Sophia, a building that began life as an Orthodox Christian church before its conversion into an Islamic mosque. Today it is a museum to Turkish history and culture.

The Hagia Sophia dates back to the year 537 CE, when the Eastern Roman emperor Justinian ordered the construction of a new basilica over the ruins of a former church, which itself was about 200 years old. The architect Isidore of Miletus deserves credit for designing and building the huge church that has withstood the ages, requiring 10,000 builders to finish the project. At the time of its construction, it was by far the largest building on the planet, incorporating marble and stone from all over the Mediterranean. The Islamic conquest by the Ottoman Empire in the 1400s led to the Hagia Sophia being converted to a mosque, with minaret towers added to the exterior. Turkey made the great building a museum in 1935, and today it receives over 2 million visitors each year.

The Hagia Sophia, once a mosque, is now a museum, seeing more than 2 million visitors each year.

The Tornado Tower resembles a Chinese finger trap with its curves of white steel and blue glass.

RIDE THE TORNADO TOWER, QATAR

A visitor to the Tornado Tower can probably think of several things that the modern Qatari skyscraper resembles. A tornado, certainly, but also a Chinese finger trap or perhaps even a nuclear cooling tower. The curves of the beautiful white-steel and blue-glass building slim down as it rises and then expands, creating an hourglass shape that is one of the most unique designs in the world. But it's not just unique, it's also efficient, because the design makes the building quite lightweight and thus able to stand without extensive structural support.

Construction on the Tornado Tower was finished in 2008 under the guidelines of the Qatari-based CICO architecture firm. Compared to some other monster buildings in Qatar and the Middle East, it's relatively modest in size—it's only the 25th-largest building in Qatar, at just 640 feet (195 m) in height. However, it won the 2009 Council on Tall Buildings and Urban Habitat Best Tall Building award for the Middle East and Africa.

BENI HAMMAD FORT, ALGERIA

Drive a few miles away from M'Sila in Algeria and you run the risk of vanishing into the Sahara Desert. That was nearly the fate of the Beni Hammad Fort, the ruins of a capital city and fortress built by the Hammadid emirs in the year 1007. Constructed by the son of the emir who founded the capital city of Algiers, Beni Hamad was meant to be a place of great splendor. Rivers fed the city's gardens, a four-mile wall protected the inhabitants, and one of the oldest mosques in Africa served the Islamic faithful.

Beni Hammad, however, was not to last. The city was abandoned in 1090 because of the threat of invasion from the Hilalian peoples of northern Africa, and then demolished for its stone and timber about 50 years later. The most famous building that remains is the ruins of the Lake Palace, a complex with a pool measuring about 150 by 200 feet (45 by 61 m), with a ramp for boats and fountains, that may have been the largest in northern Africa.

The Beni Hammad Fort is a group of ruins of a capital city and fortress in Algeria.

In 1967, the government moved the Great Temples of Abu Simbel and its statues in an effort to protect it from flooding. Pictured here, workers reassemble the pieces of the statues.

had good reason to celebrate, having recently won a major battle at a place called Kadesh against the Hittite Empire, famous for its lethal war chariots. Ramses's temple pays homage to this victory, portraying the king on his own war chariot, leading the charge against the foe and literally smiting the enemy.

The Ramses temple has another one right next to it, dedicated to his wife, Nefertari, although her temple (and her own four statues outside it) is much smaller. One of the most interesting facts about the temple is modern rather than ancient, however. When the Egyptian government built the Aswan High Dam, it ran the risk of flooding this priceless historical artifact. The Egyptian government undertook a major effort to move each brick of the temple, piece by piece, uphill to drier land. The effort was a success, and visitors can now come to the temple and look up into the face of Ramses, whose legacy has survived long after him.

ROCKING OUT WITH RAMSES IN EGYPT

Nobody who is alive today speaks ancient Egyptian or worships their gods. Nevertheless, Egyptian culture has persevered for thousands of years, long outlasting the ancient Egyptians themselves, because the Sahara Desert has preserved their buildings, their tombs, and their pyramids. Yet the most notable Egyptian relic is not the pyramids nor the sphinx but rather the Abu Simbel temples, built for Ramses II some 3,200 years ago.

Ramses II chose the location of Abu Simbel, far down the Nile River from modern cities like Cairo, due to its holy location, believing it to be special to the goddess Hathor. It took 20 years for Egyptian laborers and architects to shape, haul, and place the stones needed to build the temple and its famous four statues of the pharaoh (each 65 feet [20 m] tall) seated outside. Historians agree that Ramses

At the opening of the Abu Simbel temples are four statues of the pharaoh.

rebuilt sections until it became the largest mosque in the world, capable of holding nearly 1 million worshippers at maximum capacity.

The caliphs and sultans of the medieval era added teak roofs, marble columns, and gold-foil decorations (including gilded calligraphy) to create a wondrous and beautiful monument to the Islamic faith. The huge King Fahd Gate rests on three black and white arches, surrounded by the nine separate minaret towers that the Islamic clergy use to call the faithful to daily prayers. Bronze *mashrabiya*, geometric window enclosures typical of Islamic architecture, help to keep out the sun while allowing the breeze to flow through.

Today, the Al-Haram Mosque receives most of its visitors during the Hajj, the annual Islamic pilgrimage to the site. Those who cluster into the mosque slowly make their way to the Kaaba, where they rotate around the large black stone, kissing it and praying as they go.

The Al-Haram Mosque is both ancient and modern with teak roofs, marble columns, and gold foil decorations.

The Islamic Pilgrimage

There are five pillars of the Islamic faith required of all Muslims. One of them, the Hajj, necessitates that Muslims come to Mecca at least once in their life (some do it multiple times) and pray before the Kaaba in the Al-Haram Mosque. Each year, millions of Muslims come to Mecca for this holy task. Famous American Muslims, most notably Malcolm X, have written and commented on their Hajj experience, emphasizing how the pilgrimage has helped to build a sense of community and unity.

THE HOLY SITE OF THE AL-HARAM MOSQUE

Five times every day, 1.5 billion Muslims all over the world bow down to pray toward Mecca, their holiest city. They face this city because it is the location of the Al-Haram mosque, a name that means "the forbidden," indicating its strict religious connotation and importance to the Islamic faith. At the center of the mosque is the Kaaba, the holy stone upon which the Prophet Muhammad ascended to Heaven. The Al-Haram Mosque is one of the largest buildings in the world by interior size, even though it stands only a few stories tall.

The mosque itself is both ancient and modern. The Qu'ran references the biblical figure Abraham as having built the foundation of a house upon the site. Later, the Prophet Muhammad destroyed the idols within the building and consecrated it as an Islamic mosque. Over the centuries, different Islamic rulers have built and

Muslim pilgrims pray at the Kaaba—the center of the mosque.

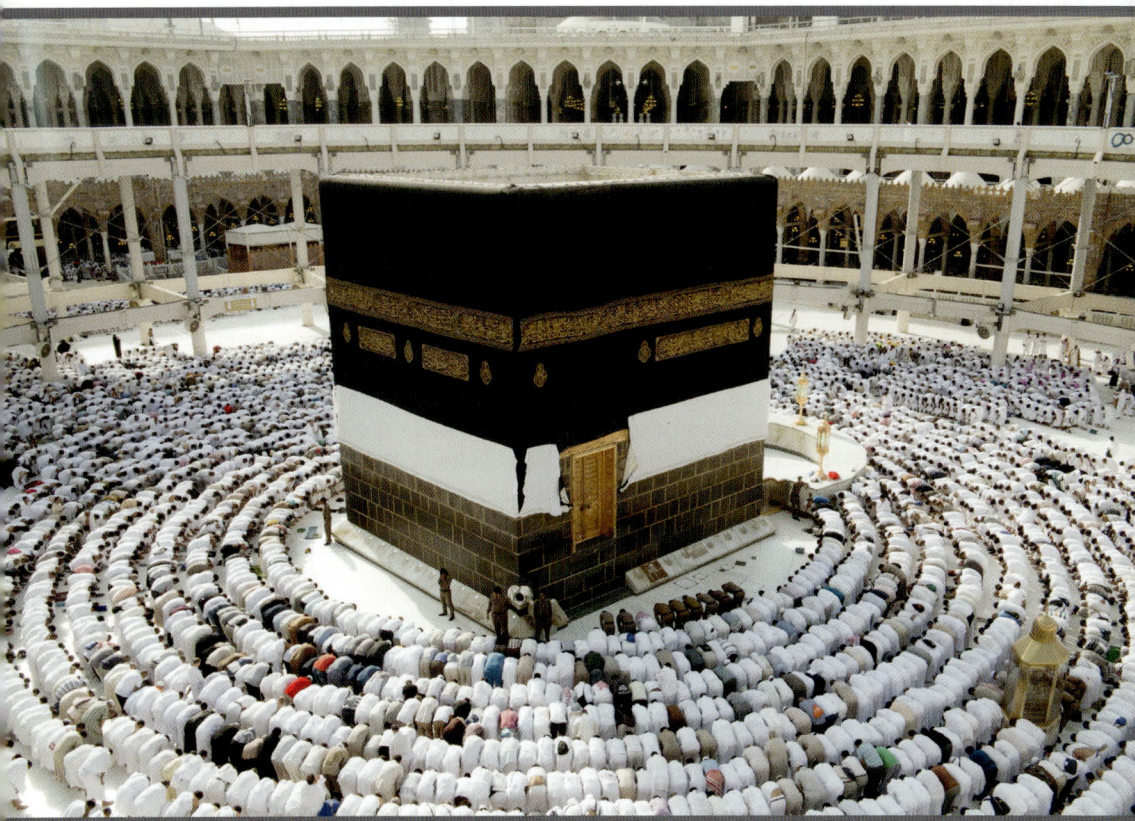

At the base of the Burj Khalifa is one of the largest fountains in the world—the Dubai Fountain.

Construction of the Burj Khalifa was part of a much larger project meant to build Dubai, the capital city of the UAE, into one of the world's great hubs for architecture, as well as science, economics, and technology. Construction began in 2004 under the helm of the U.S. architect Adrian Smith, with the expectation that it could be finished by 2009; financial woes pushed back the completion date to 2010, however, after the city had to borrow some 80 billion dollars for construction expenses.

The tower uses a post-Modern design but incorporates a uniquely Islamic design element called "setbacks," in which a large base becomes progressively smaller and smaller to support the entire building. At the base of the tower is the Dubai Fountain—one of the largest fountains in the world. The building includes an Armani hotel, residential units, corporate offices, two separate observatories, and 10 floors that house the plumbing, electrical utilities, and the machinery needed to raise and lower elevators.

TALLER THAN TALL: UAE'S BURJ KHALIFA

The Burj Khalifa uses a traditional Islamic design element called "setbacks." The large base becomes progressively smaller to support the entire building.

No structure in the history of the human race stands taller than the United Arab Emirates's Burj Khalifa (which simply means Khalifa Tower, named for Khalifa bin Zayed Al Nahyan, a member of the UAE royal family and president of the country). The building rises a whopping 2,722 feet (829 m) into the sky and features 160 separate stories of living and working space. Every fact about the building is itself a record: its 163 floors, its 2,000 vertical feet (609 m) of plumbing, its 1,600 feet (487 m) of elevator travel, and even the world's highest restaurant, "At.mosphere," located 1,450 feet (441 m) off the ground. Even though the tower was designed to resist wind forces, it still sways at the top by about six feet (1.8 m) in any direction. One of the most surprising facts, however, is that the conical design of the Burj Khalifa allowed it to use just half the amount of steel for construction (about 4,000 tons) as the Empire State Building did.

CHAPTER 5 MIDDLE EAST

During the Islamic Golden Ages of the medieval era, Middle Eastern cities like Baghdad and Cairo were some of the largest and most advanced in the world, growing the science and art of architecture. In the modern era, oil wealth has financed the building of fantastic ultramodern cities in the Middle East.

THE LIGHTHOUSE ATOP A BUILDING: PALACIO SALVO, URUGUAY

One need only crane one's neck upward to look at Uruguay's Palacio Salvo and understand why it's been called a lighthouse atop a building. It's something of a controversial building, one that can rouse both love and hatred in the hearts of architects. Italian architect Mario Palanti designed the building, which was completed in 1928, and originally did have a lighthouse that reached about 62 miles (100 km) away. At 27 stories tall, it's not as big as other Latin American structures but its Baroque style (also sometimes referred to as "eclectic style" due to the various elements) and unique tower formation make it a well-recognized landmark.

Uruguay's Palacio Salvo was completed in 1928. The lighthouse was added at a later date.

ARGENTINA'S COWBOYS AND ESTANCIAS

Cowboy culture extends far beyond the United States. Argentina is the home of another famous cowboy culture, where the gaucho herdsmen are as well known as the country's wine and tango. The famous dwellings of the gauchos, when they're not out in the countryside with the cows themselves, are the *estancias*. These beautiful plantation homes have a variety of styles, sizes, and comforts. Some are centuries old, whereas others are tourist attractions that

Gaucho dwellings sit on large plantations in Argentina.

have hot tubs and WiFi. One thing that binds them is that they are quite remote. Most were meant to be independent, self-sufficient homes for large families that might not need to go to town for months at a time.

GO CLIMB A TREE IN THE AMAZON

There are two constants in the Amazon rain forest: the rain and the trees. Put them together and you have a place where it's tough to live in a traditional house. Amazonian tribes and villages have overcome this problem by raising the stakes, quite literally. Treehouses are the norm in many parts of the rain forest, rising as high as 150 feet (45 m) into the air and allowing natives to avoid flooding as well as annoying insects at ground level. Some Amazon treehouses are lower, built on stakes so that floodwaters pass beneath the house, rather than sweeping it off its foundation.

Treehouses aren't just a kid's hideout in the Amazon. Treehouses are the norm in many parts of the rain forest, and they have solved some of the issues of living in a traditional home in the jungle.

WELCOME TO JAMAICA'S DEVON HOUSE

The Devon House is one of Jamaica's heritage sites and a national gallery for historic art and furniture.

Jamaica, like other islands in the Caribbean, was once a place where almost all blacks were slaves and almost all whites were wealthy planters. The Devon House is a testament to the historical reversal as the residence of Jamaica's first black millionaire, George Stiebel. Located in the town of St. Andrew, this beautiful Georgian mansion is today one of Jamaica's heritage sites and a national gallery for its historic art and furniture. The neatly manicured property surrounding the house, with gardens and palm trees, resembles the colonial-era plantations that made their wealth on sugarcane and salt panning.

LATIN AMERICA AND THE CARIBBEAN

CASTILLO SAN FILIPE DEL MORRO: A FORTRESS IN PUERTO RICO

The name Puerto Rico literally means "rich island" in Spanish, reflecting the ability of the Spanish to create wealth from their New World colonies—as well as the struggle against those who sought to take their wealth out from under them. To protect the capital city of San Juan, the Spanish built the Castillo San Filipe del Morro, one of the largest fortresses in the world. Originally constructed in 1539, the fortress has been upgraded and renovated through the centuries. In the 1700s, increased pressure from pirates and foreign enemies led to the construction of the massive stone walls that can still be seen today.

The Castillo turned away a variety of attackers, including the famous English privateer Francis Drake, up until the Spanish-American War of 1898. The colonial-era structure survived the bombardment of San Juan, although Puerto Rico would change hands at the conclusion of the war and become a United States territory. The U.S. military made several further refinements to the fortifications during World War II, but it has since become a tourist attraction, where the cannons are for display, not defense.

The Castillo San Filipe del Morro is one of the largest fortresses in the world.

The Notre Dame Cathedral in Port-au-Prince before its collapse in 2010.

THE OTHER NOTRE DAME, IN HAITI

When one thinks about Latin America, French isn't typically the language associated it with. However, the French, along with the Spanish, were industrious colonizers of the region, most notably in Haiti, the small nation that shares the island of Hispaniola with the Dominican Republic. The French brought not only their language to Haiti but also their architectural culture, resulting in the construction of the Notre Dame Cathedral in Port-au-Prince.

The exterior of Notre Dame was meant to resemble its Parisian counterpart, with a massive stone façade flanked by two towers. The beautiful pink and white façade of the cathedral is today in partial ruin, due to the disastrous 2010 earthquake. The lower walls remain standing, although the roof has collapsed, and architecture firms are currently planning how to rebuild the cathedral in one of the world's poorest nations. The ongoing work, headed by a Puerto Rican design team under architect Segundo Cardona, is an attempt to recreate the church's former glory.

GRAN TORRE IS CHILE'S GRANDEST BUILDING

Few skyscrapers stand out against their background quite like Gran Torre does. Located in Santiago, Chile, this skyscraper is the tallest in all of Latin America, rising 64 stories into the air and affording visitors a fantastic look at the city and the surrounding mountains. Gran Torre literally means "Great Tower," and the blue-glass structure is as great as they come. It's the second-tallest building in the Southern Hemisphere, rising nearly 1,000 feet (304 m) in height, behind only Australia's Q1 Tower. Its shadow can be as long as a mile.

The Gran Torre is the centerpiece of the Costanera complex, which itself boasts the largest shopping mall in Latin America and includes two separate hotels. It's so important as a commercial and business center that it was designed for a quarter of a million people to come and go each day. Begun in 2006 and completed in 2013, the Gran Torre was designed by Chilean engineering firm René Lagos y Asociados and built by the Salfa Corporation.

The Gran Torre represents the commercial and business center in Chile.

The Havana Cathedral once housed the remains of Christopher Columbus.

through the Caribbean. Its narrow streets, originally designed for horse carriages, open into magnificent plazas surrounded by Neoclassical and Baroque buildings. Lively colors, including pastels of pink and yellow, contrast with the wrought-iron gates and cobblestones. Many of these buildings are constructed of coral stone, which is much more readily available in the Caribbean than stones like granite or marble, and much more durable in the face of lashing cyclone wind and rain.

Five main plazas constitute Old Havana: Plaza de Armas, Plaza Vieja, Plaza de San Francisco, Plaza del Cristo, and the Plaza de la Catedral. Around them are some of the most famous buildings of the Spanish colonial era, including the Palace of the Captain-General and the Havana Cathedral, which once housed the remains of Christopher Columbus. Tourists who visit Havana today can roam through the arcades of private houses, the interior of the palaces where governors made decisions that affected the entire hemisphere, and the churches that remain a vibrant part of Cuban life today.

STROLLING THROUGH OLD HAVANA IN CUBA

The capital of Cuba, Havana played a crucial role in the Spanish colonization of the New World, beginning over 500 years ago. Founded in 1519, Havana served as a waypoint not only for Spaniards arriving in the Americas but also for the famous treasure ships stuffed full of gold, silver, and gemstones that sailed back across the Atlantic. Many pirates and enemies tried to attack the city, including the French pirate Jacques de Sores, who burned it to the ground in 1555. This event led to the construction of several massive fortresses that still stand in Old Havana, the center of the city, guarding the docks. They are among the oldest stoneworks of the Spanish colonies that still stand.

Old Havana remains in excellent condition today despite Cuba's independence from Spain, Communist revolt, and the ubiquitous *ciclón* hurricanes that plow

Old Havana is filled with colorful buildings.

Christ the Redeemer *stands above Rio de Janeiro.*

and earned consideration as one of the seven modern "Wonders of the World." Standing atop Corcovado Mountain, the statue can be seen from miles away.

Despite the intensity of Brazilian Catholicism, the impetus for the monument was a perceived "godlessness" among the general population. Donations for the construction of the monument in the 1920s came primarily from Brazilian Catholics. At the 75th anniversary of the monument's completion, the Brazilian archbishop consecrated a chapel near the statue so that faithful Christians can worship after they're done snapping photos along with the 2 million people who visit the statue annually. A restoration project in the early 2000s helped to clear away fouling and restore cracks, and *Christ the Redeemer* also enjoyed green and yellow lighting at night to support the Brazilian soccer team in the run-up to the 2010 World Cup. Although the statue was built to withstand the elements, it is a frequent target of lightning strikes, and the lightning rods in Christ's head need frequent repair and replacement.

THE TOWERING REDEEMER OF BRAZIL

The influence of Christianity throughout all of Latin America is personified by Brazil's famous statue of Jesus Christ, known as *Christ the Redeemer*. About 65 percent of Brazil's population identifies as Catholic, making it the largest Catholic nation in the world, and countless churches, monasteries, and cemeteries can be found throughout the region. As if this were not enough, the image of Christ opening his arms in a 100-foot (91 m) embrace towers over the busy streets of Rio de Janeiro. About two-thirds the size of New York's Statue of Liberty, the statue weighs 700 tons.

Christ the Redeemer is constructed from concrete and sandstone and was designed by the French-Polish sculptor Paul Landowski with the help of Brazilian engineer Heitor da Silva Costa and French engineer Albert Caquot. The Romanian artist Gheorghe Leonida modeled the face of Christ. Construction began in 1922 and concluded in 1931, at which point it became a major tourist attraction for Brazil

Christ the Redeemer *stands atop a hill with his arms wide open.*

The Intihuatana Stone, located on Machu Pichu, has been proven to be a precise indicator of the date of the two equinoxes and other significant celestial periods. It is believed that the Incas also used this for ceremonies and rituals.

The complex features a variety of different buildings, about 200 in number, including temples for worship of the sun, ceremonial buildings for official functions, astronomy observatories, and agricultural terraces that allowed the Inca to farm on the sides of steep mountains. A large square, probably used for markets, divides the residential part of the city from the agricultural past. Tourists today must hike up a steep slope to make it to the top, which is especially challenging during the rainy season, indicating the difficulty that the Inca themselves would have had getting to Machu Picchu at a time long before the invention of motor vehicles.

Incan Roads

The success of the Inca Empire was built upon their extensive road system. They laid down thousands of miles of roads throughout the Andes, linking major and minor cities and allowing fast long-distance runners to communicate from place to place using the unique *quipu* system of knots. These "talking knots" conveyed information in a similar manner as Braille letters do today, allowing Incan rulers and officials to communicate without a written language or paper. Many Inca roads and bridges remain functional today, centuries after their construction.

LATIN AMERICA AND THE CARIBBEAN

THE EMPEROR'S SUMMER HOME: MACHU PICCHU

Machu Picchu, by far the best preserved example of Incan architecture, sits 8,200 feet (2,500 m) above sea level. In its heyday of the early 1500s, the Inca Empire may have been the world's largest, both by geography and population, spread out over the Andes Mountains, which form the backbone of South America. Many Incan cities were taken over by colonization and rebuilt with new designs, however, so early archaeologists had little evidence to work with.

All this changed in 1911 with the discovery of Machu Picchu, a meeting point in Peru between the Amazon rain forest basin and the Andes Mountains. Thought to be a seasonal retreat for the Incan emperor, Machu Picchu is a city constructed out of stone that, famously, has no mortar. Each stone is precision-cut to fit into its surroundings, meaning that Machu Picchu has survived through the centuries based on the skill of its architects. Although the roofs of the buildings have fallen away, the foundations remain sturdy enough for archaeologists to study and visitors to inspect. Many mysteries remain, however, including the exact role that many buildings played in the everyday life of the ancient city.

Machu Picchu is open to visitors. Pictured here, tourists walk through the old abandoned city.

CHAPTER 4 LATIN AMERICA AND THE CARIBBEAN

Centuries of change come together in Latin America, where ancient ruins can be just miles away from colonial architecture. What's more, the contrast between the rich and the poor in Latin America means that cities may have beautiful skyscrapers as well as teeming slums.

MUSEO GUGGENHEIM BILBAO: A MODERN MASTERPIECE

Before 1997, Bilbao was a quiet Spanish city. Then the Guggenheim, a contemporary art museum, came on the scene and changed everything. Designed by the Canadian American architect Frank Gehry, it opened on October 18, 1997, to worldwide fanfare. Standing along the Nervion River, it's one of Spain's biggest museums and houses numerous works created by artists from around the world.

Generally recognized as one of the most significant works of architecture finished since 1980, the Guggenheim Museum Bilbao's wildly curving titanium exterior was created with the use of a computer drafting program that had originally been designed for the aerospace industry. As soon as the museum opened, Bilbao was transformed into an international tourist mecca.

The Guggenheim Museum is a wildly curving titanium structure that houses numerous works created by artists from around the world.

THE LOUVRE AND I. M. PEI PYRAMID, PARIS: BLENDING THE OLD WITH THE NEW

Originally a medieval fortress, the Louvre Palace became a fourteenth-century French royal residence that gradually expanded over the centuries. Although much of Europe's architecture remains rooted firmly in the past, the Louvre, now a museum, honors that history while also embracing modern design by joining the Palace with the Pyramid, a glass and metal structure in the Louvre's courtyard. Designed by the Chinese American architect I. M. Pei in 1984, the Pyramid reaches 71 feet (21 m) high, with a square base covering a surface area of 11,000 square feet (3,352 sq. m). Its outer façade contains 603 rhombus-shaped and 70 triangular glass pieces.

Although beloved today, the Pyramid was the focus of controversy during its construction and for several years after its completion, much like the Eiffel Tower. Critics had various reasons for decrying it. Some said its Modern style clashed harshly with the Louvre's French Renaissance architecture, whereas others felt its shape was an ancient Egyptian symbol for death. Still others said the structure was pretentious and immodest. Detractors also said Pei was not French and therefore unworthy of the honor to have such a project. Although the Pyramid came to be widely accepted, the structure retains its fair share of critics, who hold fast to the notion that its Modernistic style is out of place at the Louvre.

Even though many adore the Louvre today, it was the center of controversy in the past. People said that the Pyramid's architecture was too modern to go with the French Resistance style.

IN BAVARIA: GERMANY'S REAL FAIRY-TALE CASTLE

Although the iconic castle in Disney World seems to spring from a fairy tale, its real-life model is Germany's Neuschwanstein Castle. This expansive Romanesque Revival palace captures the imagination as it sits atop a rugged hill overlooking the tiny Bavarian village of Hohenschwangau. The vast structure boasts several decadent rooms, including the Hall of Singers, Throne Hall, and Drawing Room. Numerous towers pepper the top floor, with round, narrow walls that protrude from the roof, evoking the image of fair maidens awaiting rescue. Garden gates of various colors dotted throughout the property enhance the picture-book setting. Although "Mad King" Ludwig II, who ruled Bavaria from 1864 until his death in 1886, began construction in 1869, the palace wasn't finished until 1894.

European castles date back to the ninth century, when nobles built them to control and defend their lands. The structures served as military strongholds, administrative offices, authoritative symbols, financial institutions, and entertainment centers. Early castles were made of stone, wood, and mortar, with wooden fences surrounding interior courtyards called *baileys*. Stone walls eventually replaced these wooden fences and combined with outer buildings to join each palace's main structure. They, along with towers, are the key features of any European castle. It's no wonder they capture the imagination of people worldwide.

Germany's Neuschwanstein Castle resembles the iconic Disney World castle. It overlooks a tiny Bavarian village and has a wondrous mountain view, too.

The Roman Coliseum has inspired architectural designs across the world, like the Los Angeles Memorial Coliseum and the Vancouver Public Library's exterior.

THE COLISEUM OF ROME

The Coliseum sits east of the Roman Forum in the center of Rome, Italy. The largest amphitheater ever built is oval-shaped and made of brick-faced concrete, tuft, and travertine. Under the Roman emperor Vespasian, construction began in 72 CE and concluded eight years later, in 80 CE, under his son Titus. The Coliseum held an average of 65,000 spectators, who watched such entertainment as gladiator contests, executions, animal hunts, and even mock naval battles—the Coliseum could be filled with water.

    The freestanding structure was a departure from previous Greek theaters, which were built into hillsides. The Coliseum has strongly influenced architectural design over the years. In North America, it influenced the entrance to the Los Angeles Memorial Coliseum and the Vancouver Public Library's exterior. In Europe, it inspired the design of the Palazzo Della Civiltà Italiana, also in Rome, and McCaig's Tower, which overlooks the city of Oban, Scotland. Sports stadiums throughout the world have the Coliseum to thank for their stadium seating and multiple entrances, which were invented by the ancient Romans, allowing them to fill and exit the structure quickly.

THE EIFFEL TOWER: FROM CONTROVERSY TO SYMBOL OF PARIS

Today, the Eiffel Tower is a world-renowned icon of Paris, but it was not always beloved. In the 1880s, French artists and intellectuals scorned it as an industrial age monstrosity—more engineering grotesquerie than aesthetic beauty. The years since have been kinder to the tower than its preliminary critics were. Since its 1889 completion, 250 million people have visited the tower named for its architect, Gustave Eiffel.

Eiffel, a civil engineer by training, designed the 1,063-foot-tall (324 m), wrought-iron, lattice tower to serve as the entrance of the 1889 World's Fair in Paris. Today, its appeal is undeniable. For more than a century, this architectural masterpiece has captured the attention of the world, serving as a beacon of hope and love in the City of Lights and leaving its early days of controversy behind.

And here's an interesting bit of trivia: Gustave Eiffel designed the framework that supports the Statue of Liberty, which was a gift to the United States from the French government.

The Eiffel Tower is one of the main tourist attractions in Paris, bringing 250 million people there since its completion in 1889.

The Shard stands out in London's skyline and has been affectionately embraced by the public. The building stands 95 stories high and overlooks the Thames River.

energy-efficient design. Its honors include the Emporis Skyscraper Award, the Stirling Prize, and the London Region Award.

The Shard. Although the land it sits on was acquired in 1998, this supertall skyscraper took several years to complete, thanks to its unusual design and various funding issues. The developer and co-owner Irvine Sellar dreamed of the 95-story high-rise being a visually compelling vertical city that, within its walls, would encompass offices, restaurants, retail space, hotel space, apartments, and a viewing gallery open to the public. Thanks to a partnership with the State of Qatar and a design by internationally celebrated Italian architect Renzo Piano, this vision became fully realized in 2012. The innovative structure required trailblazing engineering techniques, including a first in Great Britain: top-down construction, in which the digging of foundations and building up of the core were done simultaneously.

The Shard profoundly changed London's skyline and was affectionately embraced by the public. Its viewing platform opened to fanfare on February 1, 2013. Within its first year, 1 million people visited, and notable tenants began filling the Shard's various spaces. Valentine's Day 2015 was a banner day for the Shard, with 6,161 visitors pouring 2,414 glasses of champagne.

LONDON'S MODERN ICONS: THE GHERKIN AND THE SHARD

In an ancient city with origins predating the Roman Empire, a pair of twenty-first-century architectural wonders have turned London's landscape on its ear. They have been so tightly embraced by Londoners that they have nicknames: the Gherkin and the Shard. Both infuse Modern design into London's staid architectural scene.

The Gherkin. The Gherkin is a 41-story, cigar-shaped building framed in steel and mounted on a circular floor, adorned with a glass façade of diamond-shaped panels. Commissioned by the company Swiss Re, the skyscraper was completed in 2004 under the hand of the world-renowned British architect and visionary Norman Foster. Although it was originally named the Swiss Re Building, its pickle shape propelled Londoners to dub it the Gherkin (a small pickle), which soon became its unofficial moniker. The Gherkin has won numerous accolades for its daring and

The Gherkin in London got its nickname because it is the shape of a pickle.

The Parthenon was recently under restorative construction. In 2018, the site reopened to modern-day tourists for the first time in decades.

The Parthenon replaced an earlier temple to Athena that was destroyed in 480 BCE. Its construction celebrated the ancient Athenians' military victory over Persian invaders. It took nine years to construct, starting in 447 BCE, with ornamentation added until 432 BCE.

In the mid-third century CE, a fire destroyed its roof and most of the temple's interior structure. It underwent repair in the fourth century, supposedly under the reign of Julian the Apostate, with the installation of a new wooden roof overlaid with clay tiles. This new roof sloped at a deeper incline and left the structure's wings exposed.

In the sixth century, the Parthenon was converted to a Christian church honoring the Virgin Mary. It became a popular Christian pilgrimage destination in the Eastern Roman Empire. In the 1200s, during the Latin Occupation, a tower with a spiral staircase, to serve as either a watchtower or bell tower, and tombs below the structure were added. The Parthenon remained a Roman Catholic church until the early 1460s, when the Ottoman Empire invaded Greece and turned the Parthenon into a Muslim mosque. Throughout every transition, the Parthenon remained structurally unchanged until September 26, 1687, when it became collateral damage during a Venetian bombing.

In 1975 the Greek government started restoring the Parthenon. The summer of 2018 marked the first time in decades that modern-day tourists could see the Parthenon without scaffolding.

THE PARTHENON OF ATHENS: A BEACON OF WESTERN CIVILIZATION

Located on a commanding hilltop in the center of Athens, Greece, the Parthenon is a former temple dedicated to Athena, the city's patron goddess. The most important surviving building of Classical Greece, the Parthenon is adorned with decorative sculptures that are considered the pinnacle of Greek art. One of the world's greatest cultural monuments, it's the most well-recognized symbol of both ancient and modern Greece and arguably the most famous building on earth.

The Parthenon profoundly influenced world architecture, with inventive features such as columns built with uniform sizes and styles. In addition, the roof was built with no interior support—a remarkable engineering feat that has been replicated again and again. This temple of antiquity led to an architectural resurgence during the Italian Renaissance in the fourteenth to sixteenth centuries, as Classical designs incorporated the order, lines, and purity of Greek architecture. In the mid-1800s, Neoclassical design, citing the purity of Greek architecture, further revived ancient themes. The Parthenon today inspires modern courthouses, libraries, churches, and even the White House, all of which sport columns on their exterior façades.

The Parthenon is the most important surviving building from Classical Greece.

Park Güell is filled with organic shapes and Gaudi's personal style.

Efforts to create the Sagrada Família, or Expiatory Temple of the Holy Family, began in 1862 when Josep Maria Bocabella i Verdaguer founded the Spiritual Association of Devotees of Saint Joseph. In 1874 the association started a campaign to construct a temple of atonement dedicated to the Holy Family. By 1881 it had collected enough donations to acquire a three-acre plot of land to construct the temple.

Construction started in 1882 under the architect Francisco de Paula del Villar. When Paula del Villar resigned after only a year, the 30-year-old Gaudí, an up-and-coming young architect, assumed his duties. Gaudí took over the design and made it his own, reinventing the project according to his unique vision and style, which combined Gothic and curvilinear Art Nouveau forms. Gaudí was also an accomplished engineer, drafting and calculating by hand his designs that were inspired by trees, stones, flowers, and other organic shapes.

In the first decade of the twentieth century, while still working on the Sagrada Família, Gaudí turned his attention north to Barcelona's Park Güell, where he created one of the masterpieces of his Naturalist phase. Here, as in all his projects, organic shapes inspired the architect's personal style. He created structural solutions grounded in geometric analysis for his fanciful shapes. His wildly creative and colorful ornamentation nodded to the old Baroque style, yet also broke from the classic rigidity of his predecessors.

Gaudí's innovation was a driving force for what became known as Catalan Modernism. Popular from 1888 to 1911, this flourishing period of architectural design in Barcelona would influence all the major modernist architects of the next century.

"GOD'S ARCHITECT" AND BARCELONA'S MODERNIST VISION

The Spanish architect Antoni Gaudí's celebration of nature and curved form in the nineteenth and early twentieth centuries influenced generations of architects who followed him. Gaudí's approach was so ahead of his time that his masterpiece, the Sagrada Família, is only now being completed after more than a century, with the help of computer-guided, laser-cutting technology. The Sagrada Família and six other of Gaudí's buildings—all in his hometown of Barcelona, Spain—have been declared UNESCO World Heritage Sites. Gaudí himself, a deeply religious man, has earned the title "God's Architect."

The Sagrada Família cathedral sits in the heart of Barcelona.

34 ARCHITECTURE

CHAPTER 3 EUROPE

The term *architecture* derives from two Greek terms that together mean "chief builder." It is no coincidence that European constructions over the centuries have contributed greatly to the scientific and artistic concepts of modern architecture. Many ancient structures in Europe continue to stand tall and influence today's buildings.

RYUGYONG HOTEL: NORTH KOREA'S GREAT LEGACY

North Korea's Ryugyong Hotel is a pyramidal structure that towers above the rest of the city of Pyongyang. It is one of the country's greatest achievements.

One of the poorest nations in the world, North Korea rarely appears on any list for its architectural prowess. Most buildings were constructed during the Cold War, their design a result of largess from the Soviet Union and China. However, the dictator Kim Jong-un and the Communist leadership of North Korea are determined that the capital city, Pyongyang, appears and functions like any modern metropolis.

The Ryugyong Hotel is their great achievement. At 105 stories, this pyramidal structure is by a wide margin the tallest building in North Korea. The name means "capital of willows," and its design, begun in the late 1980s, was an attempt to one-up archrival South Korea after a South Korean company built the Westin Stamford Hotel in Singapore (now called Swissôtel The Stamford), which was the world's tallest hotel when it was completed.

MONGOLIA'S YURT: THE PORTABLE HOME

The life of a nomad can be difficult, but the Mongolians have figured out a way to transport their homes with ease. The Mongolian tribes live in homes called yurts. The homes can be collapsed in just a half-hour because they are made of fabric and poles.

Few permanent cities exist in Mongolia, which is one of the last places on Earth where the majority of the people are nomadic. Most Mongolians are herders who must constantly move their horses, sheep, and cattle to new places that have fresh water and grass. They've built a perfect house to accompany them—the yurt, a portable building made of fabric and poles.

A yurt can be built or collapsed in just half an hour, with enough space for a family of up to 15 people. A pole in the center raises the short roof, allowing smoke from the central stove to escape through a chimney. Yurts have no floor; Mongolians simply cover the dirt and grass with carpets to sit, eat, and sleep.

EDO CASTLE AND JAPAN'S SAMURAI

Japan has the world's oldest monarchy, with an unbroken chain of emperors dating back over 1,000 years. Yet in Japanese history, the true power has been the shogun rather than the emperor. Edo Castle pays homage to this former military leader by demonstrating his strength and command, soaring five stories into the air with signature winged roofs and white stone walls.

Edo Castle is the centerpiece of Edo proper.

Constructed in 1457, Edo Castle became the centerpiece of the city of Edo proper, which, by the 1500s, may have been the largest city in the world. Here the shogun gave orders to his *daimyo*, his lords, who in turn used their samurai warriors to keep the peace and carry out commands. Edo Castle features a variety of defensive structures just in case the chain of command broke, including miles of inner and outer moats as well as 36 different gates. Today, it is the location of the Japanese Imperial Palace.

THE JEWEL OF KAZAKHSTAN, THE EMERALD TOWERS

The Emerald Towers (pictured to the left) are a main part of the historic city of Astana.

In the aftermath of the fall of the Soviet Union, many Central Asian nations are still looking to create their own identity. Kazakhstan is no different and aspires to be a regional and global leader as its people shape their economy and their culture in a new direction. The Emerald Towers in the historic city of Astana are a perfect symbol of this change, with their beautiful coloration and bold sloping design unlike any traditional skyscraper.

Three separate buildings make up the towers: two that rise 37 stories into the air, and one that goes up 54 stories. They are, by far, the largest buildings in both Kazakhstan and greater Central Asia. The architectural group Zeidler designed them as an homage to the steppe grasses that sway in the wind, and looking at the towers' unique bend, it's easy to imagine them swaying as well.

THE BEAUTY OF THE TAJ MAHAL

The Taj Mahal is to India what the Eiffel Tower is to France or the Statue of Liberty is to the United States. Without a doubt the most famous symbol of Indian culture and history, the Taj Mahal's beautiful white marble walls and towers are the most-visited site in all of India today. Its soaring domes, symmetrical pillars, and central onion-shaped roof make it instantly recognizable even to those who have never stepped foot in the country.

Despite its beauty, this palace is in fact a mausoleum, a place for the dead. Constructed in the early 1600s by the Mughal emperor Shah Jahan, the Taj Mahal was built after the death of his wife, Mumtaz Mahal. The emperor brought in stone-workers, carvers, and builders from throughout his empire, while also recruiting help from the Middle East and Central Asia. Though the façade of the structure itself is breathtaking, the interior is further decorated with Qu'ranic verse in Arabic calligraphy, telling the story of Mumtaz as well as the construction of the building itself.

The Taj Mahal may be beautiful but it's a mausoleum. The structure was built by the Mughal emperor Shah Jahan after the death of his wife, Mumtaz Mahal.

BOUDHANATH STUPA: A BEACON FOR TIBETANS IN NEPAL

Works of art and architecture are often associated with major historical events—whether by design or coincidence. The Boudhanath Stupa is one such example. Built in the fifth century, this huge Buddhist religious center in Kathmandu, Nepal, has today become connected with Tibetan refugees who fled there in 1959 after China invaded Tibet. The UNESCO World Heritage Site is surrounded by more than 50 Buddhist convents founded by Tibetans in exile.

A *stupa* is a domed structure built to house relics and provide space for Buddhists to meditate. This stupa, one of the largest and oldest in the world, dominates the Kathmandu Valley, both physically and spiritually. The building is constructed in the shape of a mandala, which is the physical representation of the Buddhist cosmos.

Following a 2015 earthquake in Nepal, the structure was seriously damaged, requiring the dome to be removed for safety reasons. Reconstruction began in late 2015, and the dome will now be reinforced with a steel beam through its center, known as the "life tree."

Boudhanath Stupa is linked with the Tibetan refugees who fled there in 1959—a major historical event.

SINGAPORE'S TANJONG PAGAR

The city-state of Singapore, on the southern tip of the Malay Peninsula, is home to a lot of people crammed into not a lot of space. As a result, it has one of the highest population densities in the world, with some 18,645 people per square mile (8,000 per sq. km). This, in turn, has created a constant churn of most neighborhoods as buildings are demolished for bigger and taller structures.

One neighborhood, however, has resisted the crush. The historic district of Tanjong Pagar retains many of its centuries-old structures, rickety though they may be, to display to the city's inhabitants and visitors. Tanjong Pagar means "Cape of Stakes," referencing the time when fishermen lived here before the city grew into an economic powerhouse. Legend holds that the name came from a boy who realized the city could catch shoals of swordfish by placing stakes in a way that would trap them.

The center has many historical buildings, like the famous Jinrikisha Station, a former transportation hub for the rickshaws that used to be the most practical means of rapid transit in East Asia. Duxton Hill, a former nutmeg plantation, has been turned into small shops. The AIA Tanjong Pagar building is a colonial-era structure. Rising high above them, the sole exception to the historical rule, is Tanjong Pagar Center, the tallest building in all of Singapore.

Singapore's historical building, Jinrikisha Station, is a former transportation hub for rickshaws that were once the most practical means of rapid transit.

The history of Angkor Wat is wrapped in legend. One story holds that the entire complex was built in just a single night by an architect sent from heaven. Without evidence of habitation—like old clothing, tools, or food remains—many visitors throughout history assumed it to be far older than it really is. Another persistent tale is that the god Indra ordered it built for his son.

In Khmer architecture, a wat is actually a complex of buildings assembled around the main place of worship. The area that is dedicated to the Buddha and includes the house of worship, as well as several other buildings, is the *Phuttawat*. The section that contains the monks' living quarters, kitchen, and areas open to the laity is known as the *Sangkhawat*. All of the structures are enclosed behind the same wall, even though they serve

Within the walls of a wat are other buildings, like a Ho rakhang, *or bell tower.*

different functions. The wat also has a bell tower, known as *Ho rakhang*, and the *Sala Kan Parian*, or sermon hall.

As the temples have evolved in the modern era, the monks' quarters are now essentially small apartments. These quarters are not open to the public, nor are the areas where the monks study and worship.

Several key elements of Khmer architecture and design are reflected in wats.

- *chofa*: A decoration often found on the roof of wats and palaces that resembles a tall, thin bird. These figures are thought to represent Garuda, a mythical creature that is half man and half bird and serves the Hindu god Vishnu.
- *mondop*: A traditional Thai building recognizable by its pyramid-shaped roof, supported by columns and shaped like a cube.
- *stupa*: A bell-shaped tower that includes a room often used as a relic chamber; the tower is typically ornate and covered in gold leaf.

WHAT? ANGKOR WAT, THAT'S WHAT

Perhaps the most famous buildings in all of Southeast Asia are the *wats*, building complexes constructed around a central place of worship. No wat is more famous than Cambodia's Angkor Wat, a Hindu-turned-Buddhist center of learning and faith that dates back to between the ninth and fifteenth centuries, featuring the remnants of the ancient capital of the Khmer Empire. Angkor Wat can be found in the northern Siem Reap province of Cambodia, where it sprawls over 248 square miles (400 sq. km). The ancient complex includes not just dozens of temples but also irrigation systems, roads, and villages meant to support the Khmer rulers; many modern inhabitants can trace their ancestry back to this forgotten time.

The Angkor Wat complex is a center for learning and faith filled with dozens of temples, irrigation systems, roads, and villages.

The Skybridge was built to slide back and forth, making sure that the towers sway in the wind without damaging one another.

The most recognizable feature of the Petronas Towers is the Skybridge that links them. The highest two-story bridge in the world, Skybridge is in fact not actually directly connected to the towers. Instead, it has been designed so that it can slide back and forth as the two towers sway in wind and storms without damaging either one or being damaged itself. The bridge itself rises 550 feet (167 m) above the ground, runs 200 feet (61 m) across, and weighs 750 tons. Visitors can take an elevator up to the Skybridge for a tour and selfies, but it is limited to just 1,000 visitors per day.

As the name suggests, the Malaysian oil and gas company Petronas owns the towers, fully utilizing Tower One for its business purposes. Tower Two is home to a variety of companies, from Al Jazeera to Microsoft. Due to their height, the Petronas Towers have played a role in several notable events, including the 1999 world record for BASE jumping. French climber Alain Robert twice attempted to climb the towers (with no equipment)—Tower One in 1997 and Tower Two in 2007. Robert was arrested both times without reaching the summit.

PETRONAS TOWERS: TWICE AS NICE

The crown jewel of Malaysia's capital city, Kuala Lumpur, the Petronas Towers soar 88 stories into the air, rising 1,300 feet (396 m). Their dual-tower construction makes it easy to simply refer to one as Tower One and the other as Tower Two. Construction began in 1993, and the mayor of Kuala Lumpur officially opened the towers in 1999. For the next five years they would be the tallest buildings on the planet. Designed by César Pelli, the towers are meant to be futuristic in their post-Modern style, their next-generation elevator system, and their façades inspired by Islamic art.

The Petronas Towers were completed and opened in 1999. The towers stand side-by-side at 1,300 feet (396 m) and are linked by the Skybridge.

When people are seen on the Great Wall of China, they are usually walking on the part that was built by the Ming Dynasty. It is still intact thousands of years later and stretches for 5,500 miles (8,851 km).

The wall grew in size over the next 2,000 years. Eventually, the wall that began in the area north of Beijing crossed southern Mongolia and northern China, going from east to west. The wall also began to incorporate fortresses and towers at particular intervals, as well as signal fires that were used to communicate.

The section of the wall that remains most intact today was built during the Ming Dynasty (1368–1644) in the southeastern province of Liaoning. This stretch of the wall spans 5,500 miles (8,851 km)—the entire wall is over 13,170 miles (21,196 km) long. Because of its sheer size and the fact that it has survived for thousands of years, the wall was designated a World Heritage Site in 1987 by UNESCO.

Building a Great Wall

How do you build a wall that extends over 10,000 miles? Most Chinese emperors relied on slave labor, emptying their prisons to send millions of workers north to cut, haul, and place the huge stone blocks. Legend holds that workers who perished on the project were buried within the wall itself.

ASIA

CHINA'S TRULY GREAT WALL

As the largest structure in the world, the Great Wall of China serves as a testament to humanity's ability to build. Contrary to popular belief, the Great Wall cannot be seen from space—it's not nearly wide enough, and most parts of it are about the same color as the ground it stands upon. Nevertheless, the Great Wall is by far the most recognizable symbol of China, as well as an architectural marvel with thousands of years of history.

For many centuries, China was a collection of loosely connected fiefdoms. These small kingdoms frequently fought wars with each other while remaining under threat from external enemies like the Huns and the Mongolians. The Great Wall began as a series of protective fortifications to protect these states, and at its start it was not particularly great in size.

Building began around the seventh century BCE in the area known as Chu, which was one of the largest ancient Chinese states. Stone and earth were used to construct the wall, but the builders also enlisted natural elements, such as rivers, dams, and the difficult-to-traverse mountains to aid in their efforts to provide a common defense.

Construction on the Great Wall of China began around the seventh century BCE, and work continued on it for the next 2,000 years. It is now more than 13,170 miles (21,196 km) long.

CHAPTER 2 ASIA

The largest continent in the world features many of the largest cities, from ultramodern Shanghai in China to overcrowded Karachi in Pakistan. Asian architecture ranges from glass and steel skyscrapers (among the very tallest in the world) to simple dwellings meant to be broken down as a family moves on to new places.

MUD WORKS BEST: KOUTAMMAKOU, TOGO

The mud-tower houses called *takienta* represent the national symbol of Togo, a thin nation on the Atlantic coast of northwestern Africa. The villages of Koutammakou, a region in the north of Togo, are particularly famous for *takienta* and construct them as tall as two stories. The inhabitants of Koutammakou are known as *Batammariba*, meaning "those who shape the earth." Harmony with nature is key to the design of the *takienta*, which can be rebuilt into modern homes over the remains of older mud towers worn down by weather. A *takienta*, furthermore, can be held to be sacred, meaning that those who inhabit it have a duty to keep it functional.

The Batammariba people build mud-tower houses called takienta. *They are typically two stories, and ladders are used to access the top floors.*

GADDAFI'S EGG: THE CORINTHIA HOTEL, KHARTOUM

The Corinthia Hotel in Sudan, Libya, is sometimes referred to as "Gaddafi's Egg."

Said to be one of the architectural wonders of Africa, the beautiful Corinthia Hotel resembles a Fabergé egg from far away. It has a distinctly oval design, with blue glass panels that capture the light between white concrete layers. It is sometimes referred to as "Gaddafi's Egg," because the Libyan government under Muammar Gaddafi financed it. This five-star hotel, located in the capital city of Sudan, stands at the meeting point of the Blue Nile and White Nile—hence the coloration of the building itself. Built in 2007, it has earned a variety of awards as one of the best hotels in Africa, as well as one of the most unusual architectural designs.

In the capital of Kenya stands the Britam Tower, a beautiful steel and glass, 640-foot building.

THE BEAUTY OF BRITAM TOWER, KENYA

The beautiful steel and glass Britam Tower rises 640 feet (195 m) over Nairobi, the capital of Kenya, making it the largest building within 1,000 miles. Britam has a unique modern design, resembling a prism, because its corners cross over each other diagonally as it rises. The four ground-level sides converge in a triangle shape at the top, forming just two sides at its apex. It serves as the international headquarters for the Britam Company, a financial services business, and was completed in 2017. Britam Tower includes a 12-story parking garage so that its inhabitants can find a place to park each day.

ABANDONED BY GOD: AGADEZ, NIGER

The largest city of Niger is also one of the oldest cities of the Sahara. Agadez is inhabited by the Tuareg people, a nomadic ethnic group whose name means "abandoned by God." Built in the fifteenth century by the Aïr sultan, Agadez's streets and houses have changed little over the centuries. They, too, feature the mud-brick construction that survives the desert so well, and the city's original design of 11 districts remains the layout of Agadez today. It is well known for the minaret tower of the city mosque. Standing nearly 90 feet (27.5 m) high, it is the tallest mud-brick minaret in the world.

The mosque of Agadez stands nearly 90 feet (27.5 m) high and is the tallest mud-brick minaret in the world.

A bird's-eye view of the ruins of Great Zimbabwe.

THE GHOSTS OF GREAT ZIMBABWE NATIONAL MONUMENT

Much as Timbuktu in northern Africa was a hugely important trade center in medieval times, so too was the Bantu center in Great Zimbabwe important and well connected from the eleventh to the fifteenth century. Because the climate of Zimbabwe is less forgiving to architecture than that of Timbuktu, however, the ruins of Great Zimbabwe have decayed and are no longer used by people. Nevertheless, what remains is still impressive: a major city, covering about a third of a square mile, constructed from massive granite blocks. What is believed to be a royal complex lies at the top of a hill, where six large columns decorated with birds still stand.

Many more buildings from Great Zimbabwe survive only in fragments because they were constructed from bricks made out of sand and clay. Nevertheless, they provide a great deal of insight into the ancient architecture of this region, because even modest houses boasted floors, benches, and shelves. It was believed to have hit its apex around 1450, powered primarily by nearby gold mines and growing to a population of about 10,000 people. However, this proved too large a city to be properly fed by the surrounding area, and the Bantu power in the region collapsed soon after.

AFRICA'S CASTLE: FASIL GHEBBI, ETHIOPIA

When we think of castles, we typically think of European fortresses or perhaps Japanese palaces. Yet Africa has its own castles, too, the most famous of which is called Fasil Ghebbi. Built in 1636 by the Ethiopian emperor Fasilides, the castle complex serves as a stark change of pace from previous emperors, who would move their capitals about frequently.

The Fasil Ghebbi features a 900-yard-long (822 m) wall to keep outsiders away from the many interior buildings. It boasts the castle built for Fasilides, as well as two more constructed by later emperors. There is also a separate palace, a library, a banquet room, and a chancellery for the emperor's government. Throughout the surrounding city of Gondar are monasteries and churches, baths, and even another palace built by the rulers of Ethiopia who governed from this area. Many structures in Fasil Ghebbi have a Baroque style, unusual in African architecture, due to the influence of European missionaries throughout the nineteenth century.

The Fasil Ghebbi castle was built in 1636 by Emperor Fasilides. The castle has a library, banquet room, and chancellery for the emperor's government.

THE CLIFFS OF THE BANDIAGARA ESCARPMENT

A huge series of sandstone cliffs rise over the Bandiagara Escarpment of Mali, forming a natural barrier that offers protection from storms, sun, and flash floods. A number of different ethnic groups throughout Mali's history have enjoyed this protection so much that they established permanent settlements, building entire villages out of the sandstone rock.

The first settlers of the Bandiagara, the Tellem, would bury their dead in niches in the sandstone cliffs. They inhabited the natural cave formations up until about 600 years ago, when a new ethnic group called the Dogon moved in and began to create much larger settlements. Over the centuries, the Dogon built nearly 300 separate villages out of the sandstone, carving each building and its living space from rock and living in them up until today.

A Dogon village typically has several granaries to hold food, and its people live in two-story houses called *gin'nas*. In the *gin'nas*, each generation of Dogon has carved pictorial representations of themselves into the rock, allowing them to trace their ancestry through the centuries. A large communal structure, called a *togu-na*, is a place for village leaders to gather, talk, trade, and conduct politics.

Houses sit on the Bandiagara Escarpment cliff of Mali.

AFRICA'S TALLEST BUILDING: CARLTON CENTRE, JOHANNESBURG

Johannesburg's Carlton Centre towers above the other buildings in the city. It is 730 feet (222 m) and the largest building in Africa.

Rising 730 feet (222 m) into the air, the Carlton Centre is the largest building in Africa and at one point was the tallest building south of the Equator. Today it remains one of the most important buildings for the continent's economy, because it plays host to a variety of banks, financial firms, and lending institutions. These companies all power the South African economy, the second largest in Africa after Nigeria. South Africa also has one of the most unequal economies in the world—the average worker in Johannesburg, called the City of Gold, makes about $25,000 per year. At the same time, however, half of all South Africans make just $50 per month.

The Carlton Centre itself took seven years to build, although it opened for business a full year prior to the completion of its construction in 1974. The center has a simplistic Art Deco style with little panache. It extends 50 floors from ground level to roof. The top level, called the Top of Africa, is just as popular a destination for tourists as the top of the Empire State Building in New York City. It features one of the few belowground shopping centers in the world, boasting 180 separate businesses.

At one time the center's most famous tenant was the five-star Carlton Hotel, which shut its doors in 1997 but boasted an impressive 20-year run as one of the most posh hotels in the world. The Carlton Hotel occupied 30 stories of the building, and over the years it hosted politicians like Henry Kissinger and Hilary Clinton, as well as musicians like Whitney Houston and the Rolling Stones. Recessions in the late 1990s hit the hotel hard, however, and the shipping company Transnet purchased the skyscraper in 1999 and continues its operations today. Proposals and plans to relaunch the Carlton Hotel have yet to come to any fruition.

Many of the buildings in Timbuktu have been made out of mud bricks. These types of buildings are recognizable throughout the center where some shops are located, in addition to some small villages.

ture. Nevertheless, it remains functional and still serves as a center of prayer and learning nearly 700 years after its construction.

Most of the buildings in Timbuktu have been built out of mud bricks, due to the ease of collecting the materials and their ability to withstand heat and sandstorms. These buildings, from houses to mausoleums, have survived through decades or even centuries, thanks to the hot, dry climate of the Sahara, which preserves the materials. This is the same reason that the pyramids of Egypt still stand thousands of years after their construction.

All Roads Lead to Timbuktu

Why built a big city like Timbuktu in the middle of the desert? Timbuktu was settled in the medieval era as a waypoint for caravan travelers who traded a variety of goods found through the Sahara—most notably gold, salt, elephant ivory, and peppers—with cities on the Mediterranean coastline. Timbuktu was an important stopover because of its access to the Niger River, as well as to nearby gold and salt mines. The introduction of the camel about 1,500 years ago (camels are native to Asia, not Africa) sped up the caravan routes and made Timbuktu very wealthy. However, the city today has lost much of its historical wealth and power and has a population of only 50,000 people.

TRAVELING FAR AND WIDE TO TIMBUKTU

The Djinguereber Mosque in Timbuktu was constructed in 1327 and is one of the oldest centers of learning and culture in the Islamic world.

Take a visit to the Sahara Desert and you'll quickly notice there are not many trees to be had. With a limited ability to build houses out of wood, the inhabitants of northern Africa have historically preferred mud as the primary construction material. Mud bricks are easy to make: mix dirt, water, and straw together, then let it harden in the hot African sun. Just because mud bricks aren't as ornate as concrete and steel, however, doesn't mean that they aren't practical. The ancient city of Timbuktu in Mali pays homage to the great value and resiliency of mud-brick buildings, because many that were constructed centuries ago still stand.

Perhaps the most famous building in Timbuktu is the Djinguereber Mosque. Constructed in 1327, it is one of the oldest centers of learning and culture in the Islamic world. Built by the Mali emperor Mansa Musa (considered to be perhaps the richest man to ever live), the mosque today is a World Heritage Site. It looks quite different from other mosques of the Middle East, with a flat roof rather than a dome and outside staircases rather than interior staircases. What's more, bundles of sticks from palm trees poke out at almost every angle, serving as permanent scaffolding whenever it is necessary to make repairs to the struc-

Standing next to the most prominent building in Zanzibar is the House of Wonders. The architectural design is drastically different from the Old Fort, but it is thought to be the first building in East Africa with an elevator.

Zanzibar and built their own structures to assert their authority. The most prominent building is the Old Fort, a huge garrison constructed about 400 years ago by Arabic traders who controlled the city and wanted to protect it against European attackers. Next to the Old Fort is the House of Wonders, home of the former Omani sultan; it is believed to be the first building in East Africa constructed with an elevator. The Malindi Mosque is one of the oldest mosques in all of East Africa, constructed in the fifteenth century from white stone. Nearby, an Indian trader built the Neoclassical Old Dispensary in the late 1800s to sell pharmaceuticals. European colonists contributed to the design of Stone Town with the construction of several cathedrals, both Roman Catholic and Anglican, in their efforts to Christianize the population (they failed; today, 99 percent of Zanzibar remains Muslim).

Stone Town features many architectural relics of the medieval African slave trade, including museums, former holding facilities, and public memorials. Although the African slave trade is more commonly associated with transatlantic voyages, east coast ports like Zanzibar powered an Indian Ocean slave trade until it was outlawed in the mid-1800s.

THE ROCKS OF STONE TOWN, ZANZIBAR

One of the most important cities of the entire eastern coast of Africa, Zanzibar's history dates back centuries, connecting it with trade routes throughout the Indian Ocean. Stone Town reflects this long history with buildings that are also centuries old. The name "Stone Town" itself comes from the historical use of coral stone as an ingredient in cement, mortar, and bricks. Relics of its past include narrow alleyways that long predate the use of the car and specialized stone benches called *baraza* that offer relief when heavy rains turn the streets to mud.

Features of colonialism by different powers are on display in Stone Town. Over the centuries, these different colonial powers competed for control of

The Old Fort in Zanzibar was built by Arabic traders who controlled the city and wanted to protect it from European attackers.

CHAPTER 1 AFRICA

The first dwellings in human history originated in Africa tens of thousands of years ago. Today, African architecture spans the striking contrast between ultramodern glass-and-steel skyscrapers and traditional clay-and-wattle huts, which were constructed with such a proficient design that they have not needed improvement over the centuries.

KEY TERMS

Arcade: A building or exterior construction supported by a series of arches perched upon columns.

Arch: A curved support structure that holds up weight, balanced on two sides.

Bracket: Anything projecting out of the surface of a building's exterior to provide structural or visual support.

Column: A main pillar supporting weight, composed of a base, shaft, and capital at the top that holds the ceiling up.

Dome: A half-sphere shape that usually stands at the tallest point of a building, providing stability without much material.

Eave: A roof overhang that provides protection from rain and snow.

Façade: The exterior of a building.

Fortifications: Protection of a building or city, usually referring to thick walls, but also to defenses like moats or gun slots.

Foundation: A large mass, usually of cement, meant to keep a structure in place and level.

Free-standing: A building that has no foundation as an anchor.

Grille: A panel for ventilation, often decorated.

Hut: A one-room building, typically made of simple materials, and not requiring professional design or assembly.

Lattice: A decorative panel, usually made of wood, over an exterior surface.

Masonry: Stonework.

Molding: Decorative strips of wood, stone, or clay.

Mortar: Agent used to hold bricks or stone together.

Order: Term used for classical styles of architecture.

Pagoda: A tower with multiple overhanging roof layers; most common in East Asia.

Panel: A smooth surface, often rectangular and framed by moldings.

Plaza: Spanish term for a large open space, typical throughout Spanish Empire.

Rafters: Sloping frame support for a roof, to which the roof itself is attached.

Skyscraper: Any building that has over 40 stories and/or rises 500 or more feet (152 meters) above the ground.

Spire: A tall, slender fixture on the very top of a building.

Thatch: Roofing or flooring made from straw or dried grass.

Tower: Any particularly thin and tall building.

the meeting together of two or more cultures to create a synthesis of new buildings. Finally, modern structures like the Empire State Building demonstrate that the sky is quite literally the limit when it comes to the next generation of architecture and engineering.

Names of famous architects appear whenever they deserve credit for their creations. As an example, the Danish architect Jørn Utzon designed the unique Sydney Opera House and will forever be associated with that work, even though he did not oversee the completion of the task itself. Yet for many structures, the original architect's name is forever lost to history. Indeed, some structures see each generation take it upon themselves to improve upon an ancestral design, building spirit houses, mud-brick granaries, or *gaucho* ranches one span taller or wider each time.

Several common threads link every structure found throughout the world. All structures, whether one story high or 100 stories high, must have integrity so that they stay sturdy. They retain aesthetic elements, from "vanity spires" that cause a skyscraper to exaggerate its height to the beautiful calligraphy inscribed throughout many buildings of the Islamic world. Many structures utilize a dome shape to maximize interior space while minimizing weight and building materials; both the Hagia Sophia of Istanbul and the far more modest St. Mary's Basilica of New Zealand rely on the simple, practical dome structure.

People build structures for a variety of reasons other than simple shelter. Some do it for money, others for faith, and others for pride and artistic achievement. Human structures have grown larger, taller, wider, and more complex over time, and today's ultramodern skyscrapers will doubtless look puny in comparison to the great architectural achievements of the future. Even so, these futuristic structures may still be no more practical in many parts of the world than simple structures of wood and clay.

INTRODUCTION

Every human on earth, rich or poor, must find shelter against the forces of nature. The first structures our ancestors built kept the sun out and predators at bay. With each successive generation, we stacked stones, wood, mud, and straw slightly higher or wider. Today, 1,000-foot-tall skyscrapers serve the same function as simple huts, even if they cost billions of dollars more, affording us protection, comfort, and a place to call home.

Architecture represents a unique art form because of how it must blend science, engineering, and mathematics to create a structure that will not just look good but will also endure the elements. Nobody wants their house to collapse upon them, but nobody wants to live in an ugly cube either. This forces architects to carefully choose design factors such as construction materials, location, height, and usage of any building so that it can be built without delays, survive earthquakes or high winds, look good, and even turn a profit for ownership.

No human achievement can compare in scale to modern architecture. The largest building on the planet, the Burj Khalifa of Dubai, soars over 2,000 feet (609 m) into the sky, with the steel in its foundation weighing more than three blue whales. The city of Hong Kong tops the world record list with over 300 separate skyscrapers. As the world's population increasingly urbanizes, architects must create more buildings in less space, resulting in new designs and innovations to tackle the challenges of life in the twenty-first century.

Yet the majority of the world's people do not live in ultramodern skyscrapers, and many must be their own architects. Mongolian nomads live in yurts—simple felt tents that can be set up and broken down in just an hour. The Batammariba people of Togo live in towers, two or three stories tall, constructed of mud. The Inuit lack even these basic building blocks and instead construct igloos from snow and ice to give them shelter from the fierce Arctic temperatures.

The history of architecture dates back further than history itself. Archaeologists suggest that early humans may have built shelters at the same time as the discovery of stone tools, some 2 million years ago. The first great civilizations built their own monumental structures, like the Egyptian pyramids and Mesopotamian ziggurats, to demonstrate their prowess in design and construction. The Great Wall of China, built over the span of centuries, indicates the dedication of the human race to improve upon our physical surroundings.

Many of the structures described in this book fall into one of several categories. Ancient structures, like Greece's Parthenon or Mexico's Teotihuacan, date so far back in the past that we are struck with awe that people could have built colossal pyramids or columns with hand tools of stone. Medieval buildings, like the Great Mosque of Timbuktu, indicate how architects met the challenges posed by the local environment, demanding specific design changes to better stand tall. Colonial churches and fortresses, like the *castillos* (castles) of Puerto Rico, reflect

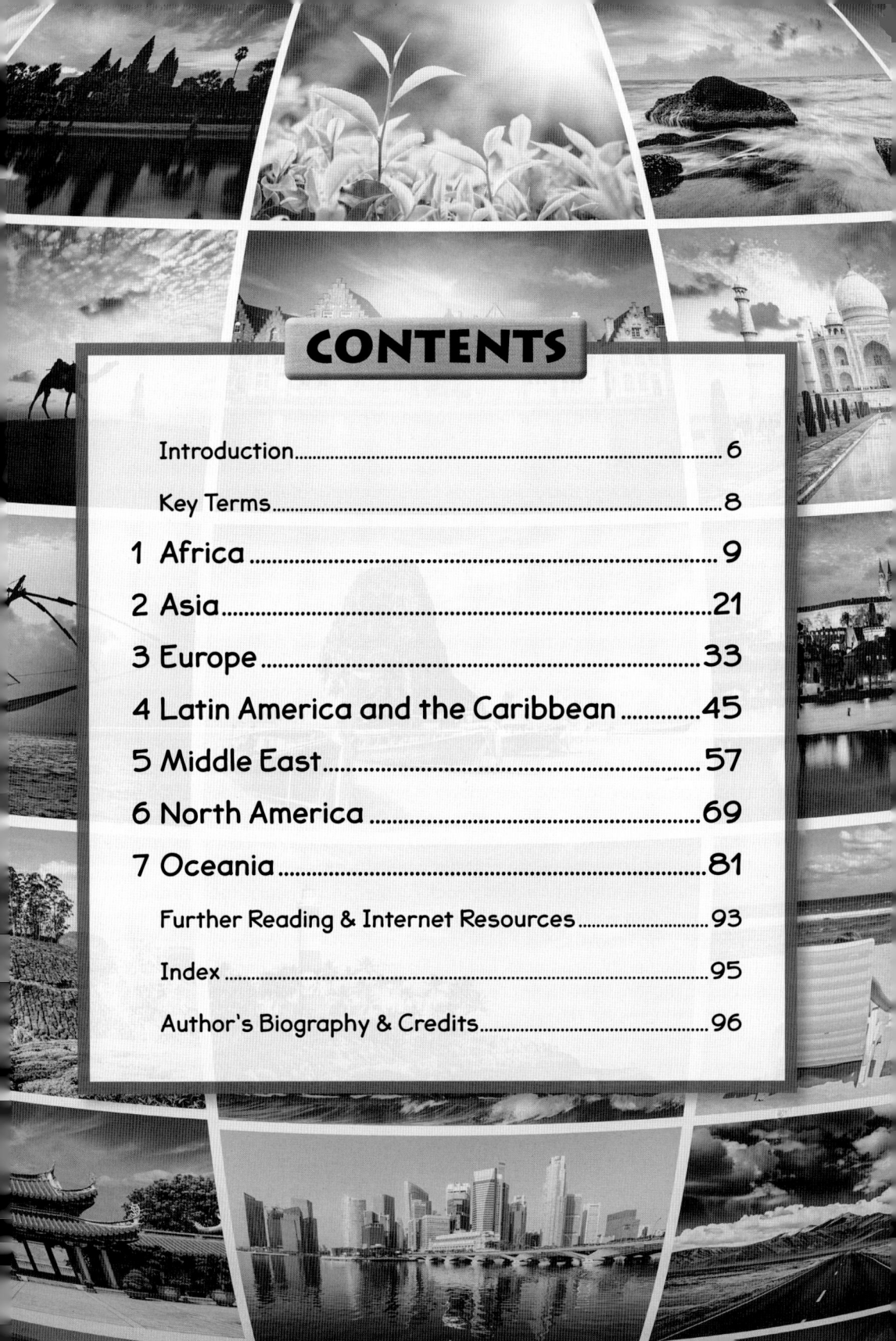

CONTENTS

Introduction	6
Key Terms	8
1 Africa	9
2 Asia	21
3 Europe	33
4 Latin America and the Caribbean	45
5 Middle East	57
6 North America	69
7 Oceania	81
Further Reading & Internet Resources	93
Index	95
Author's Biography & Credits	96

Mason Crest
450 Parkway Drive, Suite D
Broomall, PA 19008
(866) MCP-BOOK (toll free)
www.masoncrest.com

Copyright © 2020 by Mason Crest, an imprint of National Highlights, Inc. All rights reserved. No part of this publication may be reproduced or transmitted in any form or by any means, electronic or mechanical, including photocopying, recording, taping, or any information storage and retrieval system, without permission in writing from the publisher.

Printed in the United States of America

First printing
9 8 7 6 5 4 3 2 1

Series ISBN: 978-1-4222-4283-4
Hardcover ISBN: 978-1-4222-4284-1
ebook ISBN: 978-1-4222-7531-3

Cataloging-in-Publication Data is available on file
at the Library of Congress.

Developed and Produced by Print Matters Productions, Inc. (www.printmattersinc.com)

Cover and Interior Design by Tom Carling, Carling Design, Inc.

THE WORLD ART TOUR
Architecture

BY David Wilson

MASON CREST

Architecture

Clothing and Fashion

Culinary Arts

Dance

Decorative Arts

Drawing and Painting

Festivals

Sculpture

The World Art Tour
Architecture